PREFACE

The Sierra Nevada has attracted explorers, hikers, and other sightseers since it was crossed by men like mountainman Joe Walker and explorer Captain John Fremont. John Muir further proclaimed its grandeur and beauty in his writings. He was probably more instrumental than any other man in making the Sierra well-known.

Part of the appeal of the Sierra lies in the delicate beauty of wildflower meadows and natural rock gardens. The plants of these and other areas become far more interesting when we know something about them. Does this plant always grow in dry, open areas? Can pies be made from these fruits? Do deer browse this shrub? How tall does this plant grow? Where else can it be found? Knowing something about a plant and its surroundings helps you become more aware of your own surroundings.

This book was written to help you locate and identify some of the more common and conspicuous flowering shrubs and wildflowers that grow in the Sierra Nevada. Since not all of the flowers growing in these mountains could be included in a field guide, an attempt was made to choose those plants that are most likely to be encountered by the average hiker or traveler. Others might select different plants, or leave out some that I have included. The species covered here are the ones I have met most often during my travels in the pine and fir forests and the high country of the Sierra. In some cases specific plant locations are given. These are never meant to imply that they are the only places in the Sierra where the plant grows, but are only given as examples of the type of place you might encounter the plant.

Many Sierra plants, especially those growing at higher elevations, are very slow growing and fragile. When these are trampled or picked, nature requires many years to replace them. So, whether hiking alone or in a group, stay on the trail—careless hikers who cut switchbacks or scramble up steep banks often dislodge plants that took years to establish themselves. This results in erosion and may leave a permanent scar on the landscape. The lush vegetation of many meadows has been criss-crossed with unneeded paths and in other places bare dirt has replaced beds of paintbrush and lupine. Leave the mountains as beautiful as you found them —PLEASE stay on established paths and don't pick or otherwise destroy the wildflowers of Sierra meadows.

Take this book with you when you go into the Sierra Nevada and it will introduce you to many different wildflowers. Review before you go so that you will know what to look for. It will be pleasant companion for the hiker or backpacker trying to identify a certain wildflower, or the motorist who stops to climb to a mountain meadow. The flower gardens are there and beautiful displays of flowers can be seen in the meadows along the Tioga Pass Road through Yosemite National Park. Shaded glens of flowers abound within the Giant Forest of Sequoia National Park. The Lakes Basin within the Plumas National Forest, the Carson Pass area of the Eldorado National Forest, Mineral King and Quaking Aspen Meadow in the Sequoia National Forest, Onion Valley in the Inyo National Forest— these are but a few of the places alongside good roads where wildflowers abound. Sierra wildflower gardens can be found almost anywhere you look. Once you learn a few of the wildflowers in your favorite area, you'll be surprised at how many of them will greet you in a similar place just down the road.

CONTENTS

WILDFLOWERS 3

THE SIERRA NEVADA ■ *BY ELIZABETH L. HORN*

Cover photo by Kirk Horn

THE TOUCHSTONE PRESS
P.O. Box 81
Beaverton, Oregon 97005

LIBRARY OF CONGRESS
Catalog Card No. 76-633

I.S.B.N. No. 0-911518-40-1

THE VEGETATION OF THE SIERRA NEVADA

The Sierra Nevada, with its dense conifer forests, grassy foothills, open rocky vistas, and expanses of magnificent, windy high country, forms a mountain chain along the eastern border of California, crossing into Nevada where the Carson Range lies east of Lake Tahoe. The Sierra Nevada generally lies along a north-south fault line. It is a tilted block that has a gradual rise in elevation on the western slope and an abrupt drop in elevation on the eastern slope to the floor of the Great Basin. Extending nearly 400 miles, the Sierra Nevada rises gradually southward from Plumas County to Tulare County. The elevations of the mountain passes illustrate this rise toward the south: Yuba Pass (6,701 feet), Donner Pass (7,240 feet), Carson Pass (8,573 feet), Tioga Pass (9,941 feet), and Forester Pass (13,300 feet) are examples.

Plant distribution depends greatly on precipitation and temperature. Because the Sierra Nevada lies in the path of the prevailing Pacific winds, most of the moisture is dropped on the western slope, leaving the eastern slope much drier. In the high country, this comes in the form of snow, which, as it melts, provides a fairly constant supply of water during the growing season.

The Sierra flora is a mixture of species that also grow in the Cascade Range and Rocky Mountains, together with plants related to those occurring in the western lowlands and eastern deserts surrounding the southern Sierra. This is a relatively young mountain range and has extensive alpine areas. The alpine flora is composed of a relatively small group of arctic-alpine plants that are cosmopolitan (mountain sorrel is a good example) and a larger group of endemic plants, which are found nowhere else (sky pilot is a good example).

Greatly influenced by the patterns of temperature and precipitation, the vegetation of the Sierra Nevada can generally be grouped into several zones or belts. On the lower western slopes, usually called the foothills, are found brushlands (chaparral) and mixed oak and pine woodland. Above this are montane and subalpine coniferous forests, merging at higher elevations with alpine areas where the growing season is too short and climate too severe to allow a continuous tree cover. These zones are also found on the eastern slope, but are much narrower and are altered by drier conditions. Each of these zones will be described, along with its dominant or most conspicuous vegetation.

The warm, lower western slopes comprise the foothill zone, whose vegetation consists of grasslands, scrub growth, and open woodlands extending up to about 5,000 feet elevation. Various species of oak, pine, ceanothus, and manzanita dominate. Often a colorful display of wildflowers occurs during the spring, while most of the plants become dormant in the summer. Only those species that extend into the coniferous forests at higher elevations will be treated in this book.

The montane forest lies at 3,000-6,000 feet elevation in the southern Sierra, 4,000-7,000 feet elevation in the central and 5,000-8,000 feet in the southern Sierra. Summer temperatures are warm, but not as hot as in the foothill zone, and occasional summer showers bring relief. Sometimes referred to as the transition or yellow pine zone, the lower elevations of this zone are characterized by ponderosa pine *(Pinus ponderosa)*, sugar pine *(P. lambertiana)*, and, in drier sites, Jeffrey pine *(P. jeffreyi)*. Douglas fir *(Pseudotsuga menziesii)* becomes important in the northern Sierra, while sugar pine and Jeffrey pine are more plentiful in the upper part of the zone. White fir *(Abies concolor)* is often the most common tree species in the upper part of the zone. The giant sequoia *(Sequoiadendron giganteum)* forms groves at the lower portion of this zone, up to altitudes of about 6,000 feet. Extending from the central Sierra southward, its best growth occurs in the southern Sierra.

The subalpine forest has a very short altitudinal range, in many places being only about 1,000 feet. Depending on latitude, it is found from 6,500 to 9,500 feet elevation. The subalpine forest is controlled by a cool climate consisting of wet winters and dry summers with short growing seasons. Red fir *(A. magnifica)* eloquently described by John Muir as "charmingly symmetrical," is the most important species found in this zone. Often occurring in dense stands to the exclusion of other species, it dominates large areas of the Sierra forest. Sparse stands of western white pine *(P. monticola)* are scattered throughout. Lodgepole pine *(P. contorta)*, grows along meadow borders, white fir *(A. concolor)* in the lower portions of the zone, and mountain hemlock *(Tsuga mertensiana)* extends into the upper reaches of the zone.

Timberline occurs near 7,000 feet in the northern Sierra and near 11,000 feet in the southern Sierra. Above timberline is the alpine zone, characterized by open, rocky expanses. The most common conifers at timberline are the whitebark pine *(P. albicaulis)*, juniper *(Juniperus occidentalis)*, and, toward the south, foxtail pine *(P. bal-*

fouriana). The alpine tundra, while more extensive than in the Cascade Mountains to the north where it occurs only on the highest peaks, is not continuous throughout the Sierra. The crest of the range is cut by numerous gaps or passes which dip below the elevation required for the alpine zone. For instance, the continuity of the alpine zone is broken for about 3 miles at Tioga Pass. The crest is interrupted for about 20 miles at Mammoth Pass, about 25 miles south of Tioga Pass.

The eastern slope of the Sierra is much more precipitous than the western slope. Although it has similar zones, these are greatly condensed due to the smaller area and more abrupt change in elevation. The red fir forest is also found in the Carson Range east of Lake Tahoe and in local areas of the northern Sierra. The subalpine forest is represented mostly by small patches of lodgepole pine. Jeffrey pine is the most important species of the montane zone represented on the eastern slope. Scrub forests of pinyon *(Pinus monophylla)* and juniper represent the foothill zone. Bitterbrush, sagebrush, and rabbitbrush also represent the scrub zone, although these species extend nearly to timberline.

None of these zones is clearly delineated. Each merges imperceptibly into adjacent zones. Rocky outcrops, slopes, moist swales, and meadows all occur within these zones and greatly influence the plants growing there. The great latitudinal and altitudinal range found in the Sierra produce a wide variety of habitats and plant communities, each with its own characteristics.

HOW TO USE THIS BOOK

More than 300 species of wildflowers and flowering shrubs are discussed in this book, with some 200 pictured in full color. Identification of wildflowers is often difficult, especially for the novice. However, since flowers do tend to grow in specific areas, or habitats, the wildflowers presented in this book have been grouped according to where they *most likely* will be discovered. Thus, when you find a flower that is unfamiliar to you, rather than leaf through the entire book, check its location—is it growing in a rocky crevice? A gravelly slope? Along a bubbling stream? In a wet meadow? On a river bank? In the shade of a red fir?

The plants treated in this book are grouped into one of four areas—or habitats.

Section One: shaded or open conifer woods. Many wildflowers grow in forests where they are sheltered from intense temperature changes and drying wind and sunlight. The pyrola, orchid, wild gin-

ger, Solomon's seal, and violet are good examples of plants most often encountered in shaded forests.

Section Two: dry forest openings, rocky bluffs, sunny roadsides, forest borders, and grassy meadows. Dry openings occur in all of the forested zones of the Sierra and many species growing on mid-elevation rocky slopes also occur in similar areas at timberline. The manzanita, stonecrop, and penstemon are examples of wildflowers requiring warm, dry, sites.

Section Three: wet areas, moist meadows, streams, pond margins, and damp swales. Since much of the Sierra Nevada is rather dry, water exerts a profound influence. Streams, for instance, may have lush vegetation along their banks, while the forest floor a few feet away lacks herbaceous cover. Wet areas, whether in sunny openings or within shaded woodlands, often have a greater variety of wildflowers than other areas. Elephant-head, ladies' tresses, camas, buttercup, marsh marigold, bistort, and lily are only a few of the flowers found in this section.

Section Four: timberline and above. This section includes those wildflowers found mainly above timberline, either on open, rocky ridges or in meadows surrounding cascading streams of snow melt. Because so much of the southern Sierra Nevada consists of rocky basins, and rocky areas· below timberline produce similar conditions, only those species most typically encountered above timberline are included in this section. Wildflowers commonly encountered below timberline as well as above will be found in one of the other three sections.

Many wildflowers that bloom in the spring in the foothills are found in early summer in the lower reaches of the montane zone. However, many are not. Only those foothill species that normally extend into the montane zone are included here.

Most plants typically fall into one type of area; others, however, occur in more than one area. Others may grow on a site that *appears* to clearly fall into one of the above sections, even though the area really is a composite of more than one habitat type. Therefore, you may have to make a second or even a third choice! For instance, a shaded pine forest may be quite dry and rocky, producing an environment closely resembling an open, dry slope. Or, a timberline wildflower may occur at a slightly lower elevation where conditions are favorable. A dry meadow may have been covered with several feet of water earlier in the season. Nonetheless, most of the wild-flowers treated in this book will be easily found in the appropriate section.

The flowers are arranged by family within each section so that those resembling each other will be grouped together. Comparison of the plant to the photographs and the written description should make identification fairly easy.

To make your hike or picnic in the Sierra even more interesting, try studying the book first and get acquainted with it. Then take it with you and see how many of the flowers shown here you can find in their natural setting.

ABOUT SCIENTIFIC NAMES AND COMMON NAMES

Most wildflowers have more than one common name, depending on the locale where they grow, their medicinal or functional use, or a variety of other factors. Therefore, common names are often quite confusing. Even the beginning botanist should attempt to learn the scientific names of the plants he encounters, simply because the scientific name is more likely to be standardized.

For instance, the Washington lily is called the Shasta lily in northern California; the names cat's ear, sego lily, mariposa lily and star tulip are all used for members of the Calochortus genus, and these names are often used interchangeably; the names sky rocket, foxfire, and scarlet gilia all are the same wildflower. There are many similar examples. A scientific name, however, can only be used for one plant. *Oxyria digyna,* commonly called mountain sorrel, refers to the same plant, whether it grows in the Sierra, the Rocky Mountains, or in the northern mountains of Europe or Asia.

Two words make up the scientific name of every plant. The first is the generic name or genus name, the second is the specific or species name. In our example, *Oxyria* is the genus name and *digyna* is the species name. These words are usually derived from Greek or Latin names and may, therefore, seem strange to us. Nonetheless, they often tell us something about the particular plant. The name *Oxyria,* for instance, comes from the Greek *oxys,* which means sharp or sour and refers to the acid juice that gives the plant a sharp, acid taste. Other names are also descriptive, such as *triphylla* which means three-leaves, *occidentalis* which means western, or *striata* which means striped. Some names commemorate a famous botanist or naturalist. *Purshia tridentata,* the scientific name for bitterbrush, honors an early American botanist, Frederick Pursh. The specific name *tridentata* describes the three-toothed leaf tip.

ACKNOWLEDGMENTS

Many persons, knowingly or unknowingly, contributed to this volume by being helpful and encouraging along the way. They made this book much easier and enjoyable to produce.

Many offered knowledge about their local area—and of the wildflowers that grew there. Chuck Telford of Quincy introduced me to new areas of northern California; Lillian Mott of Grass Valley pointed me to good wildflower hunting around Donner Pass; Mrs. Paul DeDecker suggested good botanizing places in the southern Sierra. Forest Service and National Park service officials were extremely helpful in supplying maps, information and directions for my explorations. Although it would be impossible to mention them all, a few deserve a special thanks. Edwin Rockwell of the Inyo National Forest, Gordon Heebner and Ted Stubblefield of the Sequoia National Forest and Owen Evans of the Tahoe Basin Management Unit. Bob Fry of Yosemite National Park and Dick Burns of Sequoia Kings Canyon National Parks both suggested numerous areas within their parks for finding wildflowers. Both National Parks offered their library and herbarium facilities for study and plant identification. I am especially grateful for the help of Dr. Carl Sharsmith of Yosemite National Park. He graciously shared his knowledge and observance of Sierra flora.

Finally, there were those who kindly consented to reading the manuscript. Dr. Kenton L. Chambers of Oregon State University, John Thomas Howell of the California Academy of Sciences, Dr. A. A. Lindsey of Purdue University, and Dr. Carl Sharsmith. Their suggestions and aid greatly improved the clarity and readability of the original manuscript.

My husband Kirk was both encouraging and helpful, aiding in the selection of photos and doing many other tedious tasks.

To all of these people, I am grateful.

E. L. H.

IDENTIFYING SIERRA CONIFERS

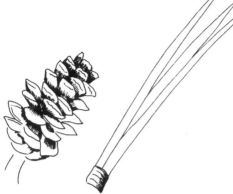 

Pines: needles in bundles or clusters, usually held together by a thin sheath
woody cones with thick scales

True Firs: needles single, leaving a small round scar when falling from twigs
cones always erect on branches, scales drop off, leaving central core of cone

Whitebark Pine *(P. albicaulis)*
5 needles per bundle
cone scale without prickles
near timberline

Foxtail Pine *(P. balfouriana)*
5 needles per bundle
cone scale with small incurved prickle
upper elevations on dry, rocky slopes

Western White Pine *(P. monticola)*
5 needles per bundle
cones slender, 4-10 inches long
subalpine forest

Sugar Pine *(P. lambertiana)*
5 needles per bundle
cones slender, 10-20 inches long

Ponderosa Pine *(P. ponderosa)*
3 needles per bundle
cones 3-6 inches long
cone scale turned outward
montane forest

Jeffrey Pine *(P. jeffreyi)*
3 needles per bundle
cones 6-12 inches long
cone scale turned inward
dry rocky slopes of montane forest, especially
on eastern slopes of Sierra Nevada

Lodgepole Pine *(P. contorta)*
2 needles per bundle
cones round, 1-2 inches long
subalpine forest

Pinyon Pine *(P. monophylla)*
1 needle per bundle
cones 1-2 inches long
dry, rocky slopes, mostly on eastern slopes of
Sierra Nevada

Red Fir *(Abies magnifica)*
needles somewhat 4-sided
cones 4-8 inches long
subalpine forest

White Fir *(A. concolor)*
needles flat
cones 2-5 inches long
montane and subalpine forests

Douglas Fir *(Pseudotsuga menziesii)*
needles borne singly
cones with 3-parted bract
montane forest

Giant Sequoia (*Sequoiadendron giganteum*)
needles scalelike, thickly covering branches
cones 1 to 2 inches long
montane forest of central and southern Sierra
  Nevada

Mountain Hemlock (*Tsuga mertensiana*)
needles single, arranged around the stem for
  bushy effect; leader at top of tree "droops"
cones 1-3 inches long
subalpine forest

Western Juniper (*Juniperus occidentalis*)
needles scalelike
"cone" a purple, berrylike fruit
dry slopes and ridges, mostly on eastern
  slopes of Sierra Nevada

SECTION I

SHADED
AREAS

WILD GINGER
Asarum hartwegii
BIRTHWORT Family

Wild ginger is an interesting plant. To find it you must look for the heart-shaped leaves amid the duff and debris of the forest floor. These deep green leaves, 3 to 6 inches wide, are beautifully patterned along the veins. The stems emerge from a scaly rootstock and are usually prostrate, the leaves being 3 to 6 inches above the ground. The flowers themselves are dull purple or maroon and also grow close to the ground. The most conspicuous features of the flower, however, are the triangular, hairy lobes, which taper into a tail that may extend an inch or more.

A similar species, *Asarum lemmonii,* found in moist areas, also has thin, heart-shaped leaves, but lacks tails on the flower lobes. Although it is found in most of the central and northern Sierra, it is not nearly as common as *A. hartwegii.*

The rootstock is extremely aromatic, accounting for the reference to ginger in this plant's common name. An eastern species of *Asarum* is reputed to have been used by the early settlers as a ginger substitute. The ginger of commerce is prepared from the branching rootstocks of the common ginger of Asia and New Guinea, *Zingiber officinale,* which belongs to the Ginger Family, not the Birthwort Family.

Range: Sierra Nevada north into southern Oregon.

Wild Ginger

10

MINER'S LETTUCE
Montia perfoliata
PURSLANE Family

The dainty flowers of this purslane are characterized by five quarter-inch pale pink or white petals, and two green sepals. This miner's lettuce, is most easily recognized, however, by the arrangement of the two small leaves on the otherwise bare stem. These are united to form a saucer or cup one-half or two inches in diameter beneath the cluster of flowers. Four to ten inches tall, miner's lettuce is found in brushy areas along most streams and on the floor of ponderosa pine and red fir forests wherever it is shady and damp. The flowers bloom from April to June.

As the common name implies, the miners who swarmed the foothills in their quest for gold found this plant to be very valuable. It was used as a salad green not only by the miners, but also by the early settlers and, even earlier, by the Indians. The raw leaves are quite good to nibble as you walk along a quiet mountain path.

Range: Lower California north to British Columbia, east to North Dakota.

Miner's Lettuce

CALIFORNIA INDIAN PINK
Silene californica
PINK Family

Also called catchfly and campion. Growing 6 to 24 inches tall, this brightly-flowered plant is one of the most colorful in the Sierra. The flowers are a brilliant scarlet and about 1 to 2 inches wide. Five petals, each deeply-cut into four lobes, further accentuate this flower's beauty. These tattered edges may remind you of the cuts made by a "pinking" scissors and thus help you remember the common name.

Another diagnostic trait of this pink is the sticky secretion found on the upper part of the stem. Small insects often are enmeshed in the material. This gives rise to the common name, catchfly. California Indian pink is found in lower elevation pine forests. It blooms in the early part of the summer even though it may also be found during August in some areas.

More than a dozen pinks are found in the Sierra Nevada. While the California Indian pink may be the most conspicuous, two others deserve mention. *Silene sargentii* grows in crevices and rocky areas at upper

Miner's Lettuce

California Indian Pink

elevations throughout much of the Sierra. It has white or rose-colored flowers and the petals are divided into two lobes, with each lobe having a small lateral lobe, instead of four equal-sized lobes. It is a tufted plant and grows only 4 to 5 inches tall. The flowers appear in July and August. Another species found in rocky areas and dry slopes at higher elevations is *S. montana.* Its flowers are greenish white or tinged with red, and each flower lobe is deeply cleft into 4 or 6 lobes. Commonly called mountain campion, it grows from 6 to 18 inches tall.

Range: Southern California north to southwestern Oregon.

WESTERN BLEEDINGHEART
Dicentra formosa
FUMITORY Family

Found in moist, shady woodlands at moderate elevations, bleedingheart is easily recognized—the pale purple or pink flowers consist of four petals which form a heart-shaped sack. The leaves, too, are distinctive, each being finely divided, resembling a lacy doily or fern leaf. You'll find these

lovely flowers blooming during the spring and early part of the summer, although in some sheltered places they may linger to the end of July.

You may also encounter two other species of *Dicentra* while exploring the Sierra Nevada. Golden-eardrops has yellow flowers as its species name *chrysantha* (golden) implies. These bright-colored spires are abundant on dry slopes and invade disturbed sites such as roadsides or burned areas. The coarse stems grow 2 to 6 feet tall. The loosely-clustered heart-shaped flowers are erectly perched on the stems, instead of hanging like those of *D. formosa.* Golden eardrops are found from the foothills up to about 5,000 feet elevation, from the central Sierra Nevada to lower California.

Steers head *(D. uniflora)* has small pink or white flowers which have the over-all appearance of a steer's head. It's found in wet, rocky places up to timberline.

Range: Central California north through the Pacific states to British Columbia.

Western Bleedingheart

Steers Head

Golden Eardrops

BANEBERRY
Actaea rubra
BUTTERCUP Family

This perennial herb has an erect stem 1 to 3 feet tall, with large leaves divided three times. The white flowers are in a round-topped cluster at the tip of the stems and have a dainty appearance, largely because of the long slender stamens. Actually, the fruits or berries are almost as conspicuous as the flowers. They are a bright shiny red or white, the latter form correctly deserving the common name doll's eyes.

Baneberry can be found in moist woodlands. In the southern Sierra, for instance in Sequoia National Park, it blooms in May and June. Farther north it blooms later in the season. Mid-July will find its flowers in the shaded forests around Harden Lake and Morrison Creek in Yosemite National Park. The shiny berries appear about a month after the flowers.

Range: Widespread in North America.

BROWN'S PEONY
Paeonia brownii
BUTTERCUP Family

Growing in scattered clumps in open woodlands, these plants reach 10 to 20 inches tall and have large, thick peony flowers that are fairly inconspicuous when they bloom in May and June. Their leathery, dull brown or reddish petals form a globular cup, but fall off soon after the flower appears. The stems grow 1 to 2 feet tall, but often bend over when mature so that the seed pods actually rest on the ground. The leaves are somewhat succulent and are irregularly divided into narrow lobes.

This species of *Paeonia* was discovered by the explorer-botanist David Douglas in 1826 in the Blue Mountains of Oregon. Cultivated peonies are derived from Asiatic and European species of this genus.

Range: California north to British Columbia and east to Nevada and Wyoming.

Baneberry

Brown's Peony

STICKY CURRANT
Ribes viscosissimum
SAXIFRAGE Famliy

Also called hairy currant. A bushy, spineless shrub, this currant has reddish bark that sheds easily. The leaves, young shoots, and berries are usually glandular—if you press a leaf between two fingers, it will cling to your skin. This trait is reflected in the specific name *viscosissimum,* a Latin word meaning very sticky. The flowers are pink, dull green, or white and the alternate leaves are 2 to 3 inches wide and shallowly three-lobed, with scalloped edges. The black, seedy berries are ripe in August or September, and, although they have very little pulp, are eaten by birds, bears, and small rodents. You'll find sticky currant beneath lodgepole and ponderosa pine as well as in forest openings.

Wax currant, also called squaw currant *(Ribes cereum),* is a 3 to 5 foot tall shrub with round leaves. The specific name *cereum* is derived from the Latin for waxy and refers to the waxy glands on the leaves. The hanging, tube-shaped flowers are pink, pale green, or even white. The berries are bright red, about a quarter-inch in diameter, and fall from the stalk when ripe in mid or late summer.

Sierra currant *(R. nevadensis),* which grows among ponderosa pine in damp places and along streambanks at moderate elevations, has small rose or deep red tubular flowers. It is a sparsely branched shrub, 3 to 6 feet tall, with flaky bark on the older branches. The berry is a deep blue or black.

Range: Widespread in the mountains of the western states.

MOUNTAIN MISERY
Chamaebatia foliolosa
ROSE Family

Also called bearmat, bear-clover, fernbush, tarweed, and kit-kit-dizzy. Mountain misery is a low-growing, resinous shrub with evergreen leaves. It grows in small patches or extensive mats in the partial shade of the ponderosa and sugar pine forests of the western slope of the Sierra Nevada. In some areas, it may be the only undergrowth, its extensive root system and

Wax Currant

Sticky Currant

dense foliage making it difficult for other plants to become established. One to two feet tall, the tangled undergrowth is hard to walk through and the sticky, strong-smelling resin clings to clothing, accounting for the common name, mountain misery.

Five-petaled white flowers, clustered at the ends of the young shoots, bloom in the early part of the summer and can be seen in June and July along the roadside near the Big Oak Flat entrance to Yosemite National Park.

Range: Sierra Nevada to northern California.

MOUNTAIN ASH
Sorbus scopulina
ROSE Family

Mountain ash is a conspicuous shrub wherever it occurs in the Sierra. In June it is adorned with flat-topped clusters of white flowers. Later in the summer and early fall, the leaves turn a beautiful red and the flowers are replaced by bright orange or scarlet berry-like fruit.

Two species of mountain ash may be found in the Sierra. *Sorbus scopulina* grows up to 12 feet tall and its leaves have 11 to 13 leaflets. It is also found in the Cascade and Rocky Mountains. *Sorbus californica* only grows 3 to 6 feet tall and has leaves with 7 to 9 leaflets. It is restricted to the mountains of northern and central California and western Nevada. Both species occur on damp, wooded slopes and canyons.

Where mountain ash is common, it may be an important food plant, as the tender twigs are known to be eaten by both domestic animals and wild game. The ripe berries are also used as food by many species of birds. Gregarious stellers and gray jays will quickly consume the fruit of an entire tree.

Range: Sierra Nevada northward into British Columbia; also in the Rocky Mountains.

Mountain Misery

Mountain Ash

15

REDBUD
Cercis occidentalis
PEA Family

Any traveler in the Sierra foothills between February and April will probably encounter a shrub covered with small pink, deep rose, or even purple-colored flowers. You might look for it if you go to Ash Mountain in Sequoia National Park. This is redbud, a shrub that usually grows from 10 to 20 feet tall. The small flowers appear before the leaves, which are 2 to 3 inches long and nearly a perfect heart-shape. When the leaves first appear, they are a coppery color; later they become shiny green. The flowers grow in clusters along the stems, and each is about one-half inch in length. These are replaced by oblong pods, which are a dull red when mature, and remain on the tree part of the following winter.

Range: Sierra Nevada of California north to the Siskiyou Mountains of southern Oregon, east to Utah and Texas.

MEADOW HOSACKIA
Lotus oblongifolius
PEA Family

Also called deervetch and meadow lotus, this colorful component of woodland edges and moist areas is recognized by its yellow flowers, adorned with a white keel. The keel is a common feature of the flowers of this family (see page 46 for a general description of pea flowers). The *Lotus* genus is characterized by pinnately-compound leaves, composed of smooth-edged (or entire) leaflets and pea-like flowers. Growing 11 to 20 inches tall, this *Lotus* has leaves with seven to eleven narrow or linear leaflets. The yellow and white flowers appear in clusters of one to five from May to August. The inch-long pods are shiny and black.

A closely related species *(L. crassifolius)* grows in drier areas. Commonly called broad-leaved hosackia, its yellow flowers are marked with red. These grow on plants 2 to 3 feet tall and bloom from May through August. The conspicuous pods may be 2 inches long and are green at first, turning a light brown or reddish color upon maturing. The gray-green leaves have 9 to 15 thick

Meadow Hosackia

Redbud

oblong leaflets.

Both of these species occur at middle elevations.

Range: Sierra Nevada and Coast Range.

PACIFIC DOGWOOD
Cornus nuttallii
DOGWOOD Family

Although several species of dogwood occur in western North America, the Pacific dogwood is by far the showiest when in bloom. This small tree is associated with forested areas and edges, where it occurs singly or in small groups, especially in moist or damp places. In the Sierra it is common on woodlands dominated by ponderosa or sugar pine. The flowers are extremely small and form green button-like clusters, found in the center of the large, showy, white bracts, which many people mistake for the flowers themselves. A bract is actually a modified leaf. In the Pacific dogwood, these egg-shaped bracts number four to six for each flower cluster and are 2 to 3 inches long. Flowering normally occurs from April to June, depending on elevation and latitude. In some areas a second flowering occurs in the fall. The leaves often turn a brilliant red in the fall, rivaling the display of springtime white. The shiny, berrylike red fruits that appear in the fall are also conspicuous, adding color to the autumn forest.

The generic name *Cornus* comes from the Latin for horn and refers to the hardness of the wood. John James Audubon, the famous ornithologist, named the plant *nuttallii* in honor of Thomas Nuttall, the naturalist and botanist who visited the West Coast collecting numerous new plant specimens. It was during his stay in 1825 at Ft. Vancouver on the Columbia River that Nuttall distinguished the Pacific dogwood from the eastern dogwood, recognizing it as a separate species.

Range: Pacific states, from California north to Idaho and British Columbia.

Pacific Dogwood

17

WHITE-VEINED PYROLA
Pyrola picta
HEATH Family

Several species of pyrola inhabit the Sierra. They vary from a few inches to a foot or so in height. The cup-shaped flowers are arranged linearly along the stems and usually hang downward. In most cases, the leaves are basal, evergreen, and leathery in texture.

White-veined pyrola or shinleaf is easily recognized by its distinctive leaves. The basal leaves are 1 to 3 inches long and a rich, dark green color. The veins, however, are marked by white. The flowers are cream or green-colored and are found at the upper part of the 4 to 12 inch stems. You'll find this little pyrola blooming along forested trails and shady spots from June to August.

One-sided pyrola or sidebells *(P. secunda)* is sometimes found alongside. It gets its name because all of the pale green or cream-colored flowers hang from or turn towards the same side of the stem. Growing about 6 or 8 inches tall, it is often overlooked because of its inconspicuous flowers and small size. A widespread plant, it occurs throughout North America and also in Eurasia.

Pink pyrola or wintergreen *(P. asarifolia)* has a long creeping rootstock, with broad, rounded leathery leaves 2 to 3 inches long. The leafless stems are 8 to 16 inches tall and bear 5 to 20 pink or red flowers with ¼ inch long oval petals. Found in moist shaded areas at middle and lower elevations, this pyrola ranges from the Pacific states to the Atlantic.

Range: Southern California and New Mexico north to Alaska; also in the Rocky Mountains.

PINEDROPS
Pterospora andromedea
HEATH Family

A tall, brown-stemmed plant, pinedrops is found on the floor of pine forests, where it derives its nourishment from fungi, perhaps growing in association with the roots of the forest trees. Growing 1 to 3 feet tall, this plant consists of one or more stems with hanging, bell-shaped flowers on the upper portion of the stalk. Pinedrops has no green

White-Veined Pyrola

Pinedrops

parts. The leaves have been reduced to small brown scales found along the stem. When the flowering stems first emerge, they are a rose-red color; after they have matured, the whole stem and floral remains turn brown and remain conspicuous until the following spring, when new stems have formed. The stalks are sometimes gathered in late summer or fall and dried for floral decorations.

The roots of this plant, like those of snow plant (see page 20) are closely associated with the fungi that decay dead organic material. The fungi reduce the decaying material, after which it is absorbed by pinedrops' roots. This association with fungi has allowed pinedrops to utilize a type of nutrition not used by green or chlorophyll-bearing members of the plant community.

Range: Widespread in the western states and across northern North America to Labrador and Pennsylvania; also reported from Mexico.

WESTERN AZALEA
Rhododendron occidentale
HEATH Family

A spectacular shrub when blooming at mid-elevations in June and July, this azalea is found in the shade of mixed conifer forests. It grows especially well along streambanks and moist or sheltered woodlands, where it may form dense thickets. Growing 2 to 14 feet tall, it is quickly recognized by its fragrant, funnel-shaped flowers. These occur at the tips of the branches and are 1 or 2 inches long. They are pink or white, with a large yellow blotch on the inner part of the upper lobe. Five stamens extend about an inch beyond the flower petals.

You'll see the western azalea, a common Sierra shrub, along many of the roadways penetrating the western slopes of the mountains. It lines the roadsides between Yosemite Valley and Tuolumne Grove in Yosemite National Park.

Range: Coastal Mountains and Sierra Nevada north into southern Oregon.

Western Azalea

SNOW PLANT
Sarcodes sanguinea
HEATH Family

This stout-stemmed plant attracts a great deal of attention because of its odd shape and brilliant red color, referred to by the species name *sanguinea.* The fleshy stems are 1 to 2 inches thick and 6 to 12 inches tall. The scale-like leaves and bell-shaped flowers, like the stem, are bright red. Poking up through the duff and humus of the forest floor, especially in the shade of towering red fir, snow plant resembles an emerging stalk of red asparagus. The common name is misleading. Although it blooms early in the summer, it does not normally push its way through snowbanks (unless covered with snow during an early summer snowstorm!). At elevations of 4,000 feet it begins blooming in May. At higher elevations, however, it can still be found in July.

Snow plant has always intrigued visitors to the Sierra. John Muir noted that it was admired by more visitors than any other Sierran wildflower. However, it was evidently not his favorite plant. He wrote in 1912 that it is a cold plant, standing alone and unmoved on the forest floor, even during wild mountain storms.

Like many other members of the Heath Family, snow plant lacks chlorophyll and derives its energy from dead plant material. Its roots do not even actually contact the soil in which it grows, but, instead are enclosed by a casing of fungi through which nutrients are transferred.

Range: Southern California north to southern Oregon.

CALIFORNIA HAREBELL
Campanula prenanthoides
BLUEBELL Family

Also called bellflower. Easily glimpsed in shafts of sunlight penetrating sequoia groves or ponderosa pine forests, this delicate wildflower blooms from June to September. It has erect, simple stems that have most of their leaves on the lower half. The flowers appear at the top of the stems, first as pale blue, oblong buds, then as blossoms with five reflexed floral lobes. Although the stems occasionally reach 3 feet in length, they are usually only about 10 to

California Harebell

Snow Plant

Western Long-Spurred Violet

20

20 inches tall.

Range: Sierra Nevada north into southern Oregon.

WESTERN LONG-SPURRED VIOLET
Viola adunca
VIOLET Family

Nearly every English-speaking country in the world has and loves its native violets. A few cultivated members of this family, for instance the pansy, adorn our finest gardens. All violets have five petals, arranged in a characteristic pattern. There are two upper petals, two lateral petals, and a larger, lower petal which extends backwards to form a shallow sack or spur at its base.

In the western long-spurred violet the spur of the fifth petal is very pronounced, being almost as long as the remainder of the flower alone. The flowers are a deep violet or pale blue—although a few white specimens are occasionally seen. About ½ inch or an inch in length, the flowers grow on 2 to 5 inch tall plants. The 1 or 2 inch long leaves are round or oval.

Interestingly, of the 25 species of violets found in the Pacific states, only about a fourth are blue. Most are yellow. A few are white or a combination of yellow, white, and violet. The mountain violet *(V. purpurea)*, occurring throughout the open, conifer forests of the Sierra, grows from a deep taproot and has yellow flowers. Less than 8 inches tall, this violet has spreading, egg-shaped, toothed leaves, which are often tinged with purple. The upper flower petals are also brown or purple tinged on their undersides. *Viola glabella,* another yellow-flowered species, has bright green heart-shaped leaves, with erect stems, and grows up to 12 inches tall. It graces the cool, damp floor of conifer forests throughout the Pacific states. Pale yellow flowers adorn *V. sheltonii,* which grows 3 to 8 inches tall in moist, shaded places. Its leaves are quite distinctive, being palmately divided two times, resulting in irregular, linear lobes. *Viola lobata,* occurring throughout the Sierra, also has yellow flowers and palmately divided leaves. However, the upper petals are backed with brown and the leaves have fewer, more irregular lobes, being divided only once. Only one completely

Macloskey's Violet

21

white violet is found in the Sierra. *Viola macloskeyi.* A dainty plant, only 3 to 4 inches tall, it grows in moist, boggy sites.

Range: Widely distributed across northern North America, and in the Pacific states to southern California.

JACOB'S LADDER
Polemonium californicum
PHLOX Family

Also called skunkweed. The dainty blue or violet flowers of this polemonium are often found shyly hiding in the shade of our conifer woodlands or in moist areas in the montane and subalpine forest zone. The bell-shaped blooms, about half an inch long, are at the end of 4 to 8 inch stems. The leaves are divided into ten to twenty leaflets, arranged opposite each other. It is this leaflet arrangement, reminiscent of a ladder, that gave rise to the common name. The upper leaflets are often partially joined together.

A taller *Polemonium* found in wet places in the Sierra is *P. caeruleum.* Its solitary, erect stems grow 1 to 3 feet tall and its spreading, bell-shaped flowers are an inch across.

Range: Sierra Nevada north to Washington, Idaho, and Montana.

DRAPERIA
Draperia systyla
WATERLEAF Family

Draperia is a low, spreading plant, often covering several feet with a loose mat. The paired leaves are 1 or 2 inches long and covered with soft, silky hairs. The pale purple, tubular flowers are about ¼-inch long and are on a coiled stem. Draperia grows on dry slopes within Sierra forests, from the foothills up to about 8,000 feet.

Draperia is a monotypic genus, having but one species in the genus. The coiled floral stems are typical of the Borage and Waterleaf Families (additional characters divide these groups). Draperia is the only perennial member of the Waterleaf Family with all its leaves in pairs. Other Waterleaf genera have some (or all) of their leaves alternate along the stem or clustered at the base.

Jacob's Ladder

Draperia

Range: Sierra Nevada into northern California.

FIVESPOT
Nemophila maculata
WATERLEAF Family

A bank decorated by these annuals is a sure sign of spring. They spread their beauty on moist slopes and hollows from April to July, from the foothills up to 7,500 feet. The spreading stems are 3 to 12 inches long and have opposite leaves. The lower leaves are deeply lobed, the upper ones entire. The flower itself is saucer-shaped, up to 1½ inches across. The clean, white flowers are purple dotted, with one large spot at the tip of each petal.

A rival for the springtime hikers' affection, baby-blue-eyes *(N. menziesii)* is typically a blue, saucer-shaped flower with a lighter center. However, the flower color is variable, sometimes being an overall pale blue color. Common in the foothills, baby-blue-eyes barely comes into the lower ponderosa pine forest of the western Sierra Nevada.

Several other *Nemophilas* also occur in the Sierra. They have smaller flowers and are thus easily overlooked. Nonetheless, they have a dainty beauty of their own. Perhaps the one most often found in the ponderosa pine forests of the central and northern Sierra, *N. heterophylla* is 4 to 12 inches tall and has tiny white or blue flowers less than ¼ inch across, its upper leaves are alternate, the lower ones opposite and deeply lobed. Sierra nemophila *(N. spatulata)* somewhat resembles fivespot. The white or blue flowers, although much smaller, are often dotted and sometimes have purple blotches on the floral lobes. Its weak, usually sprawling, stems are 4 to 12 inches long, and it occurs from 4,000 to 10,500 feet elevation throughout the Sierra. Occurring along the western base of the central and southern Sierra, *N. pulchella* has irregularly and shallowly lobed leaves, and deep blue or violet flowers with white centers.

Range: Western slopes of the Sierra Nevada.

Fivespot and Baby-Blue-Eyes

WATERLEAF PHACELIA
Phacelia hydrophylloides
WATERLEAF Family

The phacelias are a large and varied group, with nearly 90 species represented in California alone. They are herbaceous plants and most have bluish or white flowers. These often are densely coiled in spikes reminiscent of a fiddlehead. Only a few of the more widespread species will be treated here.

Nestled on the floor of red fir and ponderosa pine forests, waterleaf phacelia has foot-long stems which spread over the ground, or, occasionally, are erect. The silky leaves are distributed over the entire length of the stem, the lower ones being deeply lobed, the upper ones merely toothed. Pale violet or white bell-shaped flowers are in dense, terminal clusters.

Caterpillar plant *(P. mutabilis)* has flowers of varying color *(mutabilis* means varied), ranging from pale green or white to lavender. The flowers are about ⅓-inch long, crowded onto a dense coil, resulting in the common name caterpillar plant. The plants are from 8 to 20 inches tall and most of the leaves are basal. These tufted lower leaves are lanceolate or ovate, and may have 1 or 2 pairs of lateral leaflets. The entire plant is a greenish or gray color, covered with both fine and coarse hairs. This phacelia is common in light shade and rocky areas, in the montane and subalpine zones through most of the Sierra Nevada.

A phacelia found near timberline is discussed on page 117.

Range: Sierra Nevada north to Washington and east into Nevada.

STICKSEED
Hackelia velutina
BORAGE Family

Stickseeds, also known as sticktights and beggerticks, are named for their one-seeded fruits which have flat, barbed prickles, allowing them easy attachment to passersby. Stickseeds have alternate, narrow leaves that are without teeth or lobes. The flowers are five-lobed with a short tube with five scales at the throat. Many of the characteristics which determine the species deal with the fruits; nonetheless, the stick-

Waterleaf Phacelia

seed flower itself is fairly easy to recognize.

Hackelia velutina grows 12 to 24 inches tall and is a somewhat hairy or velvety textured plant. The basal leaves are oblong, from 2 to 4 inches long. The stem leaves are lanceolate, gradually reduced in size toward the upper part of the stem. The pink or blue flowers are about ½ inch across and bloom from June to early August in open woodlands. They are rather common at moderate elevations.

Hackelia nervosa is very similar. It grows through most of the Sierra Nevada and has a rough-hairy texture and quarter-inch blue flowers. A stickseed with a small white or blue flower with a yellow center. *H. sharsmithii* grows in subalpine and alpine sites around Mt. Whitney. It grows 4 to 12 inches tall. *Hackelia micrantha* is also a hairy plant, growing 12 to 24 inches tall. It has pale blue flowers and is common in moist places at moderate elevations.

Range: Central and southern Sierra Nevada.

HEARTLEAF ARNICA
Arnica cordifolia
COMPOSITE Family

Heartleaf arnica is a delightful little wildflower, found in shaded woodlands and, occasionally, amid the grasses of forest openings. The bright yellow flower heads are sometimes more than 2 inches across. The erect, somewhat sticky stems are 8 to 24 inches tall (although dwarf varieties are sometimes found), and have two to four pairs of opposite leaves, the lower ones being distinctly heart-shaped. The specific name *cordifolia* is derived from the Latin words for heart and leaf. The genus is named for the medicinal arnica, once a popular remedy for bruises, sprains, and other sorenesses, and obtained from the flower and rootstocks of a European species.

Of some 10 different arnicas found in the Sierra, heartleaf arnica, is probably the most common. Other arnicas are distinguished by differences in leaf arrangement and shape and various differences in the floral head. Arnicas are sometimes mistaken for groundsels (see pages 26 and 104) because they also have yellow sunflower-like

Stickseed

Heartleaf Arnica

heads. However, arnica leaves are opposite each other on the stem, while those of groundsels are alternate.

Another Composite with yellow, sunflower-like flower heads and opposite leaves, *Whitneya dealbata,* may also be confused with arnicas. However, its leaves are covered with fine hairs, giving them a silver color. Growing 10 to 20 inches tall, its flower heads are 2 or 3 inches across. Named for the pioneer state geologist of California, Josiah Whitney, this showy flower is not especially common. It is endemic to California and grows in dry openings within the montane and subalpine forest, in the central and northern Sierra.

Range: Sierra Nevada and Coast Ranges north to Alaska; also in the Rocky Mountains.

SINGLE-STEMMED GROUNDSEL
Senecio integerrimus
COMPOSITE Family

Known as groundsels, ragworts, and butterweeds, the *Senecio* genus is extremely large, with nearly 40 species occurring in California alone. The name *Senecio* comes from the Latin *senex,* meaning an old man, and is generally assumed to refer to the white hairs on the seeds. Groundsels are usually recognized by a series of characteristics. The bracts below the flower head occur in a single row. The leaves are arranged alternately on the stems, although in a few species they are mostly basal. Groundsels could be confused with some species of *Arnica* (see page 25). Both have yellow, sunflower-like heads. However, arnicas have stem leaves that are opposite each other, not alternate. *Senecios* requiring moist areas are noted on page 104.

This Senecio is a common component of the forest community, being found in the partial shade of ponderosa pine and lodgepole pine forests, from foothill areas to timberline. A stout-stemmed plant from 1 to 3 feet tall, most of its leaves are clustered at the bottom of the stem, being greatly reduced in size on the stem itself. The flower heads, about an inch wide, have both ray and tubular flowers. They bloom from May through August, depending on elevation.

A bushy, shrubby groundsel which grows

Single-stemmed Groundsel

from 3 to 4 feet tall, creek or Douglas groundsel *(Senecio douglasii)* is a foothill species, occurring in dry washes and sandy places. The linear-lobed leaves are gray or white. The yellow flower heads bloom from June to October.

Range: Sierra Nevada and northern coastal mountains of California, north into Oregon.

STAR TULIP
Calochortus nudus
LILY Family

This low-growing plant, nestled amid fallen pine needles, catches one's eye. Growing barely 6 inches tall (although some specimens are a bit taller), this star tulip has narrow, grass-like leaves and erect, white or pale purple flowers, with rounded petals. The flowers are more open than those of the mariposa lilies discussed on page 72 which have bowl-shaped flowers, more closely resembling the cultivated tulip. A very similar species, *C. minimus,* which is more common in the central and southern Sierra, has nodding flowers with pointed petals.

The name *Calochortus* comes from *kalos,* meaning beautiful, and *chortos,* meaning grass, and refers to the beautifully-flowered plant with grass-like leaves. The species name *nudus* means naked and refers to the lack of hairs on the inside of the petals— most species of *Calochortus* have a cluster of hairs at the base of the petal.

Range: Northern and central Sierra Nevada.

FALSE SOLOMON'S SEAL
Smilacina racemosa
LILY Family

False Solomon's seal is recognized by its plume of small white flowers at the end of an erect, unbranched stem. This stem grows 1 to 3 feet tall and is fairly common in shady woods at moderate elevations. The flowers bloom from April through June, depending on elevation, and are followed by red berries.

The common form found in the Sierra has clasping leaves and is designated as *Smilacina racemosa* var. *amplexicaulis, (amplexicaulis* meaning the leaf base clasps the

Star Tulip

False Solomon's Seal

stem).

Often growing nearby, star-flowered Solomon's seal *(S. stellata)* has a smaller, more dainty cluster of flowers that contains fewer blossoms. The leaves clasp the stem, which grows 1 to 2 feet tall. The berries in this species are also red. Often star-flowered Solomon's seal is hidden in the brush of moist swales or streambanks.

Range: Mountains of California, north to British Columbia and eastward to the Atlantic coast.

SPOTTED CORAL-ROOT
Corallorhiza maculata
ORCHID Family

Coral-root derives its nourishment from the decaying material of other plants rather than producing its own sugar as green plants do. Coral-root stems range in color from brown or yellow to purple. The leaves have degenerated into small scales along the length of the stem. The underground stem is divided into short, knobby, rock-like sections, responsible for the common name as well as the genus name. There are prob-

ably 15 different species of coral-root in temperate North America. Two that are common in the Sierra Nevada will be discussed here.

Growing 8 to 30 inches tall, spotted coral-root *(C. maculata)* has its flowers arranged loosely along the upper portion of the stem. This species is distinguished by the pattern on the lower lip of the flower. The white lip is three-lobed and spotted with purple. Spotted coral-root is quite common in damp conifer forests, and can be found blooming on the floor of sequoia groves in July. At higher elevations, it appears among the needles beneath mountain hemlock in early August. Not quite so common but with a showier flower, striped coral-root, *C. striata,* is found in woodlands at moderate elevations. This coral-root grows up to 20 inches tall, and has flowers that are white or pink, with purple striping.

Range: Widespread in the Pacific states, east across North America to Newfoundland.

Spotted Coral-root

Striped Coral-root

28

RATTLESNAKE PLANTAIN
Goodyera oblongifolia
ORCHID Family

A low rosette of deep green, leathery leaves, each with distinctive white markings, quickly identifies the rattlesnake plantain. Because they are evergreen, these leaves may be seen at any time of the year the ground is free of snow. The waxy, white flowers are on the upper portion of a slender stalk that grows about 12 inches tall. Found in dense, shaded, conifer forests at lower and moderate elevations, this orchid often forms small colonies.

Although not plentiful in temperate North America, the orchid family is one of the largest known. Found mainly in the tropics where many species are epiphytes growing upon tropical trees, the family has some 15,000 species. Many different orchids have been grown by florists and others to improve their large, showy flowers. The family is economically important in other ways, too. Extract of vanilla is derived from the pods of the vanilla orchid.

Range: Widespread across northern North America and in the western U.S.

SECTION II

DRY AREAS

Rattlesnake Plantain

29

GOLDEN CHINQUAPIN
Chrysolepis sempervirens
BEECH Family

A bushy, evergreen shrub, chinquapin is less conspicuous when flowering than when it has fruit. Related to the oaks of the foothills, chinquapin grows up to 6 feet high and inhabits dry, rocky ridges and slopes, where it often mingles with wild cherry, snowbush, and manzanita. The 3-inch oblong leaves are yellow-green above and yellow-gold beneath. The flowers are borne in elongated clusters or catkins and, when in bloom, can penetrate the air with their disagreeable odor. The prickly burs resemble those of the chestnut, to which chinquapin is related. They are a brownish-gold color, are quite noticeable during the latter part of the summer and make attractive additions to most floral displays.

If you take the time to dig into the chinquapin bur, you'll find a nut-like fruit, somewhat resembling a hazelnut. When ripe, usually in September or October, this nut can be very sweet-tasting. Up to three nuts may be found within a single bur; however, often only one develops.

Range: Southern California north through Oregon to Washington.

SULPHUR-FLOWER
Eriogonum umbellatum
BUCKWHEAT Family

Of the many wild buckwheats found in the Sierra Nevada, sulphur-flower is one of the most common and conspicuous. It is fairly abundant in dry, rocky places, both in the cliffs and openings of pine and red fir forests of moderate elevations and in the high country near timberline. Sulphur-flower is easy to spot: the bright yellow or sulphur-colored flowers form a compact mat over the ground. As the flowers mature they become red or pink, the dried remains turning completely brown by the end of the summer. The flower clusters are on short stalks, 4 to 12 inches tall, which rise from a many-branched woody base. Shorter, flowerless stems have small spatulate leaves.

Wild buckwheats occur in many different forms. Another common one is called nude buckwheat *(Eriogonum nudum)* because the 1 to 3 foot tall stems have no leaves. Instead, the leaves are clustered at the base

Golden Chinquapin

Sulphur-Flower

of the stem. The small white flowers, usually tinged with pink or yellow, are crowded into a ball-shaped cluster at the tips of the tall stems, or, if the stems branch, in the fork of the stems. This species of wild buckwheat is found from foothill to subalpine areas.

Oval-leaved eriogonum *(E. ovalifolium)* is a species that may occur in wind-swept timberline areas or at moderate elevations throughout the Sierra Nevada. It is a densely-matted plant, with small, half-inch leaves crowded together on short basal shoots. The oval leaves are covered on both surfaces with soft woolly white hairs, reminding one of a piece of felt. The flowering stems are only a few inches tall and carry balls of tiny cream-colored flowers, which are often tinted with red. This buckwheat is also found in the Cascades of Oregon and Washington and in the Rocky Mountains.

Range: Pacific states east to Montana and Colorado.

BITTERROOT
Lewisia rediviva
PURSLANE Family

The best known Lewisia is the bitterroot *(L. rediviva)*. It is very widespread in the western United States, growing in stony slopes, gravelly benches, and rocky crevices, and may vary in color and size from one location to another. It is a low-growing, succulent herb, with large conspicuous blossoms in the spring. The numerous sepals and petals, all looking somewhat alike, are one half-inch to an inch in length and range in color from rose or purple to pale pink or white. When blooming, bitterroot appears to lack leaves entirely. Actually, the linear leaves usually dry up and shrivel by the time the flowers open.

Yosemite bitterroot *(L. disepala),* sometimes considered a variety of *L. rediviva,* blooms in June and July on the rocky rims above Yosemite Valley. It is also called two-sepaled lewisia because it has two conspicuous petal-like sepals. The flowering stems are shorter than the fleshy, linear leaves, and each bears a single white or pink flower composed of two sepals and

Bitterroot

Nude Buckwheat

five to seven petals.

Lewisias are usually renowned for their large, showy flowers. (Two alpine species with modest blossoms are discussed on page 110) Kellogg's lewisia is quite an attractive wildflower, with its thick spatulate leaves and conspicuous, cream-colored flowers. The blossoms, tucked among the leaves, are sessile and have a pair of sepal-like bracts. The sepals themselves are oblong, with toothed margins. Kellogg's lewisia is found on sandy ridgetops and bluffs within the subalpine and montane forest zones of the Sierra Nevada.

Range: Widespread in mountains of western states.

PUSSYPAWS
Calyptridium umbellatum
PURSLANE Family

Anyone who explores the Sierra in mid-summer will undoubtedly see pussypaws. This common plant flourishes on the dry sandy soils and gravels found along trails and roadsides. Pussypaws responds to the warmth and light of the sun. In the morning and evening hours it will hug the earth, its reddish stems pressed flat against the ground. By mid-day, the stems will be nearly upright. At lower elevations, the prone plants may be 8 to 10 inches across, while at higher elevations they are much smaller, being only 2 to 3 inches in diameter. The pinkish flowers are borne in dense clusters at the tips of the stems. The basal leaves, arranged flat on the ground in a rosette, have a leathery texture and are somewhat elongate in shape.

The name pussypaws seems extremely appropriate for this little purslane. If you look carefully at a cluster of flowers, you'll see that it closely resembles the furred paws of a kitten. It feels like kitten's paws, too. Cup a cluster of flowers between your thumb and fingers, and you'll feel the softness of a kitten's paw. The black, shiny seeds that appear toward the end of the summer are eagerly consumed by chipmunks and other small rodents.

Range: Mountainous areas of the western United States, north into British Columbia.

Pussypaws

PRICKLY POPPY
Argemone munita
POPPY Family

Prickly poppy is particularly conspicuous on the sunny hillsides of the east slope of the Sierra in late July and August. Look for it when you drive over Monitor Pass. A stout plant, 2 to 4 feet tall, it has prickly stems and leaves. The large flowers, however, are the most notable features. Two to five inches across, they have three to six floppy, white petals and a central cluster of yellow, orange, or red stamens, which can number from 150 to 250. When the central stamens are yellow, the massive flowers remind one of "eggs, sunny-side up."

Range: Southern California, Nevada, and Arizona.

WESTERN WALLFLOWER
Erysimum capitatum
MUSTARD Family

Wallflowers add a dash of bright color to rocky bluffs and cliffs. Although the mustard family itself is large and variable, this genus is fairly distinctive, with its showy, round-topped cluster of flowers. Two species are common in the Sierra. The most wide-spread, *E. capitatum,* is a robust, coarse plant, frequently found in stony places below 8,000 feet. The somewhat hairy stems grow 1 to 3 feet tall and carry narrow leaves that are 3 to 6 inches long. The color of the flower varies widely. Most often a bright orange, it may also be yellow, burnt red, or maroon.

Sierra wallflower, *E. perenne,* is found at higher elevations, mostly near timberline. As is true with many alpine plants, it is smaller than its lower elevation relative. It rarely exceeds a foot in height and may be as short as 4 inches. Leaves from the previous year protect the root-crown from which the stems arise. The yellow petals are a half-inch or more long, making the flowers extremely conspicuous on rocky alpine slopes. A careful look at the individual flowers of these two wallflowers quickly identifies them as members of the mustard family. The distinguishing characteristics of this widespread group of plants are discussed on page 34.

Range: California north to British Columbia and Idaho.

Prickly Poppy

Western Wallflower

SHIELDLEAF
Streptanthus tortuosus
MUSTARD Family

Mustards comprise a large group. They are widespread and variable, with many plants of economic value. Cabbage, radish, cauliflower, turnip, and rutabaga are only a few of the more commonly known garden plants belonging to this versatile family. Still other mustards fall under the category of weeds, invading wastelands and farmland alike. As a group, mustards are identified by a watery juice, alternate leaves, and a diagnostic flower. There are always four sepals and four petals, which spread opposite each other to form a cross. Indeed, the Latin name for the family is Cruciferae. There are six stamens (rarely four or two), two of which are much shorter than the other four. All mustards are a variation of this general pattern.

Shieldleaf is an unusually pretty mustard and grows 8 to 36 inches tall. The purple or yellowish flowers are about one-half inch long, with slightly recurved sepals and twisted petals, which give the flower a contorted appearance. (The name *Streptanthus* is derived from the Greek for "twisted flower," referring to the flower shape.) On the open rocky areas where shieldleaf is usually found, the clasping, round, shield-shaped leaves often attract more attention than do the flowers themselves. They are 1 to 3 inches across, and turn yellow by the middle of the summer. Shieldleaf grows from the foothills to timberline.

Other Sierra mustards are discussed on pages 33 and 112.

Range: Northern California mountains and Sierra Nevada.

STONECROP
Sedum obtusatum
STONECROP Family

This stonecrop has most of its leaves clustered in basal rosettes, which may form a mat of thick, succulent leaves. They have rounded, blunt tips (referred to by the name *obtusatum*), and are somewhat reddish in color, especially toward the end of the growing season. The 2 to 6 inch tall stems are often tinged with red and bear smaller, oblong leaves. The yellow flowers fade to

Shieldleaf

Stonecrop

pale pink or cream late in the season. This stonecrop grows in the crevices of otherwise smooth granite bluffs and ridges, from moderate elevations to timberline. Another genus of the stonecrop family is represented by *Dudleya cymosa,* found blooming on warm rocky slopes in the foothills from April to June. Commonly called live-forever, it can be recognized by its rosettes of stiff, oblong, succulent leaves, and the bright yellow-orange or pink flowers. The flowering stems are about 12 inches tall.

Range: Sierra Nevada north into southern Oregon.

BLUE FLAX
Linum lewisii
FLAX Family

The bright colored flowers of the flax greet modern Sierra explorers, just as they did Fremont, who wrote of the "common blue flowering flax," and Capt. Meriwether Lewis, for whom it is named. The flowers are in a flat-topped cluster atop leafy stems that may grow as high as 30 inches. These often occur in clumps and have narrow, linear leaves, which are about an inch long.

Although common in lowland meadows, flax also grows in coniferous timber in the mountains and even on exposed ridge-tops, such as those surrounding Sonora Pass and Donner Pass in the central Sierra.

The flax family is rather small, consisting of perhaps 100 to 150 species. However, its economic importance rates above many other families. Linen thread, manufactured from a cultivated flax, is one of the most important vegetable fibers ever known, its use dating back to the beginning of written history. The western Indians were known to have used flax fiber for strings and cords to make baskets, mats, fish-nets, snowshoes, and other items. However, it is not considered economically valuable today.

Range: Widespread in western North America.

Blue Flax

MOCK ORANGE
Philadelphus lewisii
SAXIFRAGE Family

Also called syringa. Mock orange is a widely distributed and very showy flowering shrub that grows on rocky slopes and grassy fields at lower elevations. Although not extremely common, it stands out wherever it occurs because of its clusters of fragrant white flowers. Growing from 4 to 10 feet tall, it is a loosely branched shrub with 3 inch long, opposite leaves. The beauty and sweet scent of this flowering shrub have made it a popular ornamental and earned it fame as the state flower of Idaho.

The species name honors Captain Meriwether Lewis of the Lewis and Clark Expedition. Lewis discovered the plant and collected it in 1806 along the Clark Fork River in Montana.

Mock orange might possibly be confused with creek dogwood (page 91) or bitter cherry (page 44), both of which are also shrubs with clusters of white flowers. However, creek dogwood is usually found in moist areas, not dry, rocky slopes. Bitter cherry has white flowers in round-topped clusters, and its leaves are grouped together on short twigs, instead of being opposite each other on the branches. Some botanists consider the California plants to be a distinct variety of this species. *Philadelphus lewisii* ssp. *californicus.* Others feel the differences found in the plants growing in the southern part of the range are not significant enough to warrant this designation.

Range: Sierra Nevada north, especially on the east side of the mountains, to British Columbia and Idaho.

Mock Orange

36

SIERRA GOOSEBERRY
Ribes roezlii
SAXIFRAGE Family

Nearly 15 species of *Ribes* may be found in the Sierra. Rather than giving the exact characteristics and descriptions of each, an attempt will be made to describe the general features of the group and detail the more common species. Gooseberries and currants both belong to this genus and are shrubs with simple, alternate leaves. The outer flower parts are united to form a bell or saucer-shaped disk to which the petals are attached. Gooseberries and currants are similar in appearance. One of the chief botanical differences is in the flowering stalks. These are jointed in the currants so the berry breaks away. In the gooseberry, there is no joint, so the berry remains attached. The flowers in the currant are borne in clusters while those of the gooseberry are solitary or in pairs. In addition, the stems, and, often the berries, of most gooseberries are armed with spines or prickles, while those of currants are not. The common Sierra currants are noted on page 14.

Ribes roezlii is the most common gooseberry of the Sierra. It is a stout shrub, 2 to 4 feet tall, with spiny branches. The roundish leaves, about an inch wide, are cleft into three or five toothed lobes. The flowers have purplish or rose-colored sepals and white petals. The berries, covered with long spines, are green in the early part of the summer, later turning red or purple. The flowers bloom in May and June on dry open slopes at moderate elevations or in the partial shade of red fir and ponderosa pine.

Range: Trinity Mountains and Sierra Nevada of California.

Sierra Gooseberry

DEERBRUSH
Ceanothus integerrimus
BUCKTHORN Family

Deerbrush, named because the foliage is often browsed by deer, is one of the most common species of *Ceanothus* found in the Sierra. Its thin, oval leaves are about 2 inches long. Three ribs or veins arise from the base of each leaf. Deerbrush grows 4 to 12 feet high and has fragrant flowers in showy 2 to 6 inch terminal clusters, made up of tiny blue, or, more often, white blossoms. Deerbrush is extremely common in openings and partial shade at lower and moderate elevations, blooming from April to July.

Whitethorn or snowbush *(C. cordulatus)* has white flowers in small, dense round-topped clusters, about 1 or 2 inches long, which bloom from May through July. Another distinctive characteristic is the hard point or "thorn" found at the tips of most branches. Snowbush is a flat-topped, densely-branched shrub, 1 to 4 feet high and 3 to 9 feet across. It commonly dominates areas that have been repeatedly burned, sharing the site with greenleaf manzanita (see page 52).

Another species, commonly called chaparral whitethorn *(C. leucodermis)* grows in foothill areas. Its spiny, rigid branches carry smooth, ovate leaves and pale blue or white flowers, in 1 to 3 inch clusters. It grows 5 to 12 feet tall and blooms from April to June.

Buckbrush, *(C. cuneatus),* also known as wedgeleaf ceanothus, and greasebush, grows 3 to 12 feet tall. It is a many-branched shrub with thick, wedge-shaped leaves occurring as opposite pairs along the stem. Blooming from March to May, the small white flowers are in an umbrella-shaped cluster up to 1 inch across. Most often found on dry gravelly slopes and ridges in the foothills, buckbrush also occurs on rocky openings within ponderosa pine forests. It usually forms extensive thickets.

Range: California and Arizona north to Washington and Nevada.

Deerbrush

Whitethorn

TOBACCO BUSH
Ceanothus velutinus
BUCKTHORN Family

Ceanothus is a large North American genus found mainly in the foothills and mountains of the western United States. California has 35 to 40 species, with more than 10 found in the Sierra. *Ceanothus* species are usually shrubs, although some are prostrate (see below). A few species have spiny branches (whitethorn on page 38 is a good example), but most do not. As a group, *Ceanothus* is not difficult to recognize. The blue or white flowers are in showy clusters. When these are on the tips of the branches, they are especially spectacular. The five petals of each flower are spoon-shaped, with a thin, inrolled throat and hoodlike tip. The leaves often have three prominent ribs or veins on the lower side.

Tobacco bush is one of the most widespread members of the *Ceanothus* genus, occurring in the Rocky, Sierra Nevada, and Cascade Mountains. In addition, it has a wide altitudinal range, growing from the foothills nearly to timberline. Usually occurring in small patches or extensive brush-fields, it does well in a variety of situations and exposures. It has large, shiny, evergreen leaves, which may be 3 inches long. They are three-ribbed at the base and somewhat sticky to touch. This trait accounts for another of its common names, sticky laurel. Averaging 2 to 5 feet high, tobacco bush has white, sweetly-scented flowers. These are borne in showy clusters from 1 to 4 inches long.

Range: Widespread in the mountains of the western states.

SQUAW CARPET
Ceanothus prostratus
BUCKTHORN Family

This delightful buckthorn is readily recognized by its holly-like evergreen leaves, which form a prostrate mat covering the ground. Squaw carpet's trailing branches frequently root, and form a dense ground cover 2 to 10 feet across, sometimes larger. The stiff leaves are about an inch long and small blue flowers bloom at the ends of the twigs from April to May. This low growth form protects the soil from erosion and provides a nursebed for young conifers.

Squaw Carpet

Tobacco Bush

Douglas fir and white fir benefit from squaw carpet, which protects their seeds from rodents. It also provides shade and helps hold moisture, creating a more favorable condition for seedlings than hot, open mountain slopes.

Fresno mat *(C. fresnensis)* also forms prostrate mats, although it may have some erect stems. The half-inch long, dark green evergreen leaves are leathery and finely toothed. Found at moderate and lower elevations in the central and southern Sierra, the blue flowers bloom in May and June.

Littleleaf ceanothus *(C. parvifolius)* rarely exceeds 3 feet in height. Its elliptic leaves, however, are deciduous, and have smooth edges. The pale or deep blue flower clusters bloom from June to July in lodgepole and ponderosa pine forests. It is found in the central and southern Sierra Nevada.

Range: Northern Sierra, north to Washington and Idaho.

SERVICEBERRY
Amelanchier pallida
ROSE Family

Also called shadblow, saskatoon, and Juneberry. When the serviceberry is in bloom, it is indeed a beautiful shrub. Five narrow white petals are usually twisted to give a somewhat ragged appearance to each individual flower. The oval leaves, from 1 to 2 inches long, are roughly toothed, especially on the upper half.

The round, berry-like fruits are a deep blue color, with a whitish bloom or coating. Botanically, they are similar to apples, with bits of the flower still attached to the top of each fruit. Althought many modern taste-buds consider the fruits too mealy and sweet, explorers and miners found them a welcome addition to their otherwise bland and limited food supplies. Early settlers learned to make fine jellies, jams, pies, and wines from the serviceberry. Many Indians of western North America held the plant in high esteem and the berries were a staple in their diet. Dried berries were pressed into small cakes, which were later added to stews and soups for extra flavoring. The

Serviceberry

40

dried berries were also pounded into dried meat for carrying on long trips. The small fruits are now eaten mainly by wild animals —pheasants, grouse, coyotes, and rabbits all feast on them.

In some parts of its range, serviceberry grows to be a shrub some 15 to 20 feet tall. However, on the dry rocky slopes and sunny canyons of the Sierra, it is generally only a few feet high and resembles a creeping bush more than an upright shrub.

Range: Widespread in northern and western North America.

CURLLEAF MOUNTAIN MAHOGANY
Cercocarpus ledifolius
ROSE Family

Mountain mahoganies are most conspicuous when their feathery-tailed fruits, not their flowers, are present. In fact, the genus name refers to this characteristic. The name *Cercocarpus* is derived from the Greek *kerkos,* tail, and *karpos,* fruit. The common name refers to the mountain habitat where it is normally found, usually on dry slopes or ridges, and the hard, reddish wood.

Mountain mahogany has clustered leaves which are evergreen and leathery, with edges that are rolled under. A densely branched shrub or small tree, it has small greenish or cream-colored flowers which lack petals. Growing from moderate elevations nearly to timberline, mountain mahogany blooms from April to May, depending on elevation and exposure. You'll see the silvery plumed seeds adorning these shrubs at Monitor Pass in early August, although at lower elevations mountain mahogany may be fruiting by June.

Another mountain mahogany, *C. betuloides,* is common in many foothill areas. Its leaves are not rolled inward along their edges.

Range: California and Arizona north to Montana and eastern Washington.

Curlleaf Mountain Mahogany

WILD STRAWBERRY
Fragaria californica
ROSE Family

Wild strawberries are low-growing, perennial herbs with scaly, underground rootstocks. They generally produce runners, or stolons, which creep across the ground and root at the tips, producing a new plant. Most strawberries have numerous basal leaves, composed of three toothed leaflets and long petioles. In *F. californica* these leaflets are rounded. The white flowers are about an inch in diameter and produce a sweet-tasting, small red fruit by mid-summer. At lower elevations the flowers bloom from March to June. However, a few blooms may still be found at higher elevations in July.

A similar species grows in open woods up to timberline, *F. platypetala,* is often called broad-petaled strawberry. The leaflets of this species are not as rounded as those of *F. californica.* Rather, they are quite narrow at the base so that one leaflet does not touch another.

Rarely is the fruit of the wild strawberry seen, plucked, and eaten, even though the ground in some places may be covered with white strawberry blossoms in the spring and early summer. The berries are sought so eagerly by birds and small rodents that few ever reach the human palate. Not so well known, however, is the value of strawberry leaves, which produce one of the better wild teas. Fresh leaves can be steeped in hot water or dried for future use.

Range: Northern California south to southern California and New Mexico.

OCEAN SPRAY
Holodiscus microphyllus
ROSE Family

Also called creambush. The rose family has a number of beautiful flowering shrubs (pages 15, 40, 45). This one grows at middle and upper elevations in the Sierra, sometimes at timberline. Reaching 6 feet tall, this shrub is covered with clusters of small white or cream-colored flowers. You will see it in full bloom on the dry slopes of Mineral King Valley in the Sequoia National Forest in early August. It blooms earlier at lower elevations.

Wild Strawberry

Ocean Spray

A very similar, but smaller, shrub, *H. boursieri,* grows up to 3 feet tall. It, too, is found on dry, rocky slopes at middle and upper elevations.

The two species can be distinguished by careful examination of the leaves. Those of *H. microphyllus* are spatulate in shape (see the illustrated glossary on page 123) and toothed along the top. Rarely do the teeth extend to the middle of the leaf. *H. boursieri* leaves, on the other hand, are rounded or oval and toothed along the side.

Range: Mountains of southern California, north in the Sierra Nevada to Plumas County and east to the Rocky Mountains.

DUSKY HORKELIA
Horkelia fusca
ROSE Family

Horkelia is a perennial herb with white flowers in tight, terminal clusters. The five wedge-shaped petals emerge from a cup-like base. It grows 6 to 18 inches tall and most of the leaves are basal. These are pinnately compound with 11 to 21 leaflets.

Growing in open woodlands and slopes, it is quite variable, with many closely related forms found throughout the Sierra.

The genus *Ivesia* is closely related. Its flowers, however, are yellow or white and occur in tight clusters. An *Ivesia* sometimes found growing in open woodlands and meadows with dusky horkelia is *I. lycopodioides.* Its yellow flowers are on nearly leafless stems 2 to 8 inches tall. The basal leaves, which are 1 to 3 inches long, are divided into 20 to 50 leaflets, which are in turn divided almost to the base. The tufted leaves almost resemble clumps of moss. An interestingly named wildflower is mousetails *(I. santolinoides).* The small white flowers are in open, branched clusters. The distinctive characteristic, however, is in the basal leaves. Up to 4 inches long, they are divided into many tiny leaflets and covered with dense, silky hairs, resembling a mouse's tail. Growing 6 to 12 inches tall, mouse-tails is found in open lodgepole pine and red fir forests and subalpine areas, usually in hot, dry openings.

Range: Sierra Nevada north to Wyoming and Washington.

Dusky Horkelia

Mousetails

43

BITTER CHERRY
Prunus emarginata
ROSE Family

The bitter cherry is named for the small fruits or cherries, which are intensely bitter, even when fully ripe. The white flowers occur in round-topped clusters. Dark green oblong leaves with fine-toothed edges occur alternately on the stems. The bright red cherry appears in late summer or early fall and contains juicy, bitter pulp. Although it may attain the size of a small tree, it is more often a spreading, crooked-branched shrub 3 to 10 feet tall. The bark has a distinctly cherry odor when bruised. Look for bitter cherry in open brush fields, usually in the company of snowbush, manzanita and serviceberry (see pages 38, 52 and 40).

Also blooming in April and May, the Sierra plum *(P. subcordata)* resembles the bitter cherry. However, its fruits are a reddish-purple color and the leaves are rounded. They make excellent jams and jellies. In addition, the branches may have small spine-like twigs on them. The western chokecherry *(P. virginiana demissa),* an erect shrub or small tree, also has white flowers. However, in this species the flowers are in showy, elongated clusters, which are 2 to 4 inches long. The berries are dark purple or black, with a puckery taste. These grapelike clusters of fruit are attractive as well as being utilitarian. Some parts of the plant are considered poisonous, yet the berries are favorites with many birds. Although tart, they make good jellies, jams, and wine.

Range: Widespread in the mountains of the western United States.

BITTERBRUSH
Purshia tridentata
ROSE Family

Also called antelope bush, quinine bush, and black sage, bitterbrush is a semi-erect shrub that is widely distributed in arid regions of the western states, growing from 1 to 6 feet tall, depending on local conditions. Although not generally a conspicuous plant, its yellow flowers attract a great deal of attention in the spring. The five spatulate petals and numerous stamens are rather

Bitter Cherry

Western Chokecherry

showy, each flower being about an inch across. Its mass effect creates quite a display. The clustered leaves are three-toothed at the tip, slightly less than an inch long. They are wedge-shaped, with rolled under margins. In open places on the east side of the Sierra, bitterbrush may dominate large areas. In addition, it is often the main shrub understory of open pine forests. On Carson Pass in the Eldorado National Forest it is a scraggly shrub, barely reaching a foot tall, that blooms in early July.

The generic name *Purshia* honors Frederick T. Pursh (1774-1820), a distinguished botanical explorer and author. The shrub, however, was first collected by Capt. Meriwether Lewis. The specific name *tridentata* refers to the leaves, which are three-toothed or "tridentate." Bitterbrush is an appropriate common name because of the taste of the leaves. Nonetheless, it is one of the most important browse plants in the western states, enjoyed by both domestic and wild animals.

Range: Widespread in western North America.

MOUNTAIN SPIRAEA
Spiraea densiflora
ROSE Family

The spiraeas are attractive flowering shrubs. They have simple leaves, arranged alternately on the stems. Native spiraeas have tiny flowers, crowded into showy clusters, which may be round-topped or elongated. This species has rose or pink colored flowers. Growing up to 3 feet tall, its slender stems grow close together, forming a dense, compact shrub. The flowers themselves are extremely fragrant and dainty. The stamens are longer than the other flower parts, giving a fuzzy effect to the floral cluster. Blooming from July through August, mountain spiraea grows at moderate and upper elevations, usually on moist rocky slopes. Spiraeas are showy plants when in bloom and add to the beauty of many of our mountain slopes.

Range: California north to Wyoming, Montana, and British Columbia.

Bitterbrush

Mountain Spiraea

BREWER'S LUPINE
Lupinus breweri
PEA Family

Lupines are a well-known group of western plants. Although individual species may be difficult to tell apart, the group itself is easily recognized by the palmately compound leaf (the leaflets originate from a common point, like the fingers of a hand) and the pea-shaped flowers. Lupines have alternate, usually long-stemmed leaves, which are sometimes covered with silky hair. The number of finger-like leaflets comprising the leaves varies with different species. There may be as few as four or as many as 17. The flowers are usually blue, but in some species are yellow, white, or even red. The five-petaled flower is two-lipped. The upper petal is called the banner, while the lower two petals are united to form a keel. The remaining side petals are usually called wings. Only a few of the more typical species of lupine will be treated in this book. A species found in moist areas is shown on page 89.

Brewer's lupine is a leafy, matted, often prostrate, plant, its woody stems rarely exceeding 6 or 8 inches in height. The seven to ten leaflets of each leaf are about ½-inch long, and covered by white, silky hairs. The flowers are blue or violet, with a yellow or white center, and are less than a quarter-inch long.

A similar-appearing plant, occurring on dry, alpine ridges and slopes, *Lupinus lepidus* grows in low woody tufts. Its leaflets are more acute or pointed than those of *L. breweri*. Five to six lance-shaped leaflets comprise the leaves, which are covered with flattened hairs and are mostly basal. One variety, *L. lepidus* var. *danaus,* has pale lilac or white flowers.

A much taller lupine, *L. stiversii,* is a freely branching annual growing 4 to 20 inches tall. It is usually called harlequin lupine because of its coloration—the upper petal is a bright yellow while the wings are pink or purple and the keel white. These flowers are much larger than the ones just mentioned, being three-fourths of an inch long. The hairy leaflets are about an inch long. Blooming from May to July, harlequin lupine is found in sandy and gravelly places

Brewer's Lupine

Harlequin Lupine

in the foothills and ponderosa pine forest of middle elevations.

Range: Southern Sierra Nevada, north through Washington.

SMOOTH SIDALCEA
Sidalcea glaucescens
MALLOW Family

The mallow family is well known because of the many ornamental plants belonging to the group, such as the hibiscus and hollyhock. The *Sidalcea* genus has more than 20 species, mostly in California and Oregon.

This mallow with its loosely-arranged, pink flowers, is a notable component of the plant community found on grassy slopes and dry open meadows, from the foothills nearly to timberline. Its smooth stems are 1 to 2 feet long and have leaves that are deeply lobed into five to seven narrow divisions. The pale flowers are about an inch across and appear from May to July in places such as Crane Flat in Yosemite National Park and the Pinecrest area of the Stanislaus National Forest.

A very similar mallow, checkerbloom *(S. malvaeflora)*, grows 1 to 2 feet tall and has flowers that are 1 to 2 inches wide. Its stems and petioles, however, are not smooth but have short, coarse hairs. Checkerbloom has two types of leaves, the lower ones being bluntly lobed and the upper ones being divided and toothed.

Mallows that grow in moist places are discussed on page 89.

Range: South Central Sierra Nevada to northern California; also into Nevada.

Smooth Sidalcea

47

BLAZING STAR
Mentzelia lindleyi
LOASA Family

Dancing gaily in the bright sunshine, blazing star grows best in dry, open areas below 4,000 feet, where its buttery-colored flowers add color to the drying grasses of foothill areas in late spring and early summer. This blazing star grows 6 to 24 inches high and has pinnately lobed leaves that are 2 to 6 inches long. These leaves have bristly white hairs which cling to anything they touch, giving rise to another common name, stickleaf. The five-petaled flowers are 2 to 3 inches across and each petal has a small point on its tip. The variety found in the Sierra foothills is usually designated as *Mentzelia lindleyi* ssp. *crocea*.

Mentzelia laevicaulis blooms later in the summer, usually from June through October, and is distinguished by its narrower, longer petals (a petal is 2 to 3 inches long). It grows on both sides of the Sierra, ranging up to 8,500 feet elevation, and is most often encountered in dry places. It is particularly conspicuous in the disturbed soil bordering roadways leading into the mountains. Occurring through most of the Sierra Nevada, it grows 3 or 4 feet tall, but is usually much shorter.

Mentzelia dispersa, a smaller species, is also found in dry, rocky or sandy soil at lower and moderate elevations. Growing from 4 to 16 inches tall, it has rough-feeling, lanceolate or oblong leaves that are entire, although the upper ones may be pinnately lobed. Its flowers are quite a bit smaller than those of the two species discussed above. The floral petals are ¼-inch or less and the flowers are clustered at the top of the stems.

Range: Widespread in the coastal and mountainous areas of California.

FAREWELL TO SPRING
Clarkia williamsonii
EVENING PRIMROSE Family

Blooming brightly in May, June, and July, this group of wildflowers adds color to otherwise dry openings after the native grasses have turned brown. Several species occur in foothill areas and range into the lower conifer forests, adding a splash of color along most of the roadsides leading

Blazing Star

Farewell To Spring

into the mountains. Although named for Captain Clark of the famed Lewis and Clark expedition to the mouth of the Columbia River, more *Clarkia* species occur in California than in the Northwest. The group has four-petaled pink or purple flowers. Commonly found in the foothills and lower forest areas, *Clarkia williamsonii* has purple fan-shaped flower petals. These are a lighter color near the center, with an especially dark purple splotch along the upper edge. This *Clarkia* was named for Lt. Robert Stockton Williamson, who explored the Sierra mountain passes for a possible railroad route during the 1850's. A pink-flowered species *C. dudleyana,* often grows alongside. Its fan-shaped petals are streaked with white. It grows in the central and southern Sierra foothills.

Another species, *C. rhomboidea,* has smaller diamond-shaped petals with a long claw referred to by the species name. It grows 3 to 20 inches tall and has lavender or pink flowers that are about an inch long. You'll find it on dry slopes from lower California to Washington and Montana.

Range: Central Sierra Nevada.

FIREWEED
Ephilobium angustifolium
EVENING PRIMROSE Family

Fireweed readily comes into burned over areas, sometimes covering acres with its tall stems and rose-colored flowers. It is not restricted to such a locale, however, also growing along roadsides, in fields, and in forest openings.

Usually about 3 feet tall, it may grow up to 6 feet in height if conditions are right. The brightly colored blossoms are borne on an elongated flower stalk. The flowers at the lower end bloom first, and it is possible to find unopened buds, fully opened flowers, and fruits all on the same plant. The 3 inch seed pods are four-sided. When mature, the pod splits into four linear segments, releasing seeds with tufts of white, silky hairs. These act as a parachute, transferring the seeds over great distances. Fireweed is widely distributed in the Sierra, being found on both sides of the mountains and extending up to timberline.

Fireweed is eaten by deer, elk, and domestic animals. The young shoots can also be used as a vegetable, if cooked some-

Fireweed

49

what like asparagus. In addition, the leaves, either fresh or dried, can be used to make a hot tea.

Range: Widespread in Eurasia and North America.

CALIFORNIA FUCHSIA
Zauschneria californica
EVENING PRIMROSE Family

By the latter part of August most of the wildflowers of the mountains, even those normally found at higher elevations, are spent. The leaves have shriveled and dried; stems have turned brown; fruiting pods or seeds have been blown by the wind, hopefully to sprout the following spring, when the snow has melted. The brightly-colored California fuchsia is an exception. When most other mountain flowers have set seed, this wildflower may still be found blooming on dry slopes and ridges, sometimes clinging to a rocky granite crevice. The floral tube is scarlet or crimson and about 1½ inches long. The notched, floral lobes are shorter than the stamens, which protrude from the end of the tube.

Most botanists place the higher elevation plants in a subspecies category, subspecies *latifolia*. They have broader leaves (as the name *latifolia* implies), which are gray-green and hairy. California fuchsia forms brightly colored clumps from mid-elevations to higher elevations, and may be found blooming along the rocky slopes surrounding Lake Tahoe.

These flowers often attract humming-birds, who stick their long beaks into the floral tube for nectar and the insects found within the tubes. For this reason, they are sometimes called hummingbird flower or hummingbird trumpet.

Range: Lower California (Baja) north to Nevada and southern Oregon.

SIERRA ANGELICA
Angelica lineariloba
PARSLEY Family

The angelicas are robust members of the carrot or parsley family. They are erect perennials which grow from stout taproots and have large leaves that are divided several times. Although the flowers are small, the

California Fuchsia

Sierra Angelica

floral clusters are quite large, thus making it a conspicuous plant. Two species might be encountered in the Sierra.

Sierra angelica is a stout-stemmed plant growing 2 to 6 feet tall. Its leaves are divided into numerous narrow leaflets, each from 1 to 4 inches long. The white flowers grace the dry slopes of Mineral King Valley in early August.

Brewers angelica *(A. breweri)* has much wider leaflets, which are toothed along the margins and are often hairy. It grows in the central and northern Sierra and can be found at Crane Flat and the Hetch Hetchy Valley in Yosemite National Park.

Gray's ligusticum *(Ligusticum grayi)* resembles the angelicas. It grows 2 to 3 feet tall and is characterized by large, mostly basal, lace-like leaves with toothed leaflets and white flowers. It is found throughout the Sierra.

Range: Central and southern Sierra Nevada.

YAMPAH
Perideridia bolanderi
PARSLEY Family

Waving its small rounded clusters of white flowers, yampah may be found in dry openings or washes. Quite often it grows along road shoulders, basking in the sunshine created by this artificial opening. A slender, erect plant standing 1 or 2 feet high, its stems carry only a few long leaves. These are 2 to 6 inches long and are divided several times into many linear segments, some of which are substantially longer than others.

Another Sierran yampah occurs in wet or drying meadows, *P. parishii.* It also has small white flowers in umbrella-like clusters. It differs from Bolander's yampah in leaf structure. These are divided into one or two narrow segments, which are grass-like or threadlike and may themselves be 4 inches long. Both species have edible roots. The tubers (thick, rounded underground stems) may grow up to 3 inches long and resemble small sweet potatoes. They were used extensively by the Indians for food. Captain John Fremont, who crossed

Yampah

California in 1844, reportedly ate yampah, declaring it to be one of the finest of all Indian roots. Care should always be used when seeking yampah roots, since the plant could be confused with death camas (see page 75).

These plants are sometimes referred to as Queen Anne's lace. However, this name is most correctly reserved for plants in the genus *Daucus,* the wild carrot. Most passers-by consider yampahs to be weeds and their abundance causes most viewers to ignore them. Sierra meadows enhanced with white flowers toward the latter half of the summer usually are covered with one of the yampahs.

Range: Sierra Nevada north into eastern Oregon, Utah, and Wyoming.

GREENLEAF MANZANITA
Arctostaphylos patula
HEATH Family

The manzanitas are an extremely important genus, found almost exclusively in the arid belts of California and southern Oregon, typically on dry slopes and hillsides, and usually in full sunlight. Manzanitas thrive on poor, stony soil and are well known for their ability to grow in burned areas. Many species sprout from unburned root-crowns. Manzanitas are easily identified by the distinctive character of their stems, leaves, flowers, and fruits. The stems and branches of the Sierran species are all rigid and usually crooked, with a smooth, shiny, dark red or reddish brown bark that peels off in thin strips. The leathery leaves are rarely toothed or notched. The small urn-shaped flowers are pinkish or white, and are in nodding clusters found at the ends of the branches. The fruits, especially those of the larger species, resemble miniature apples—in fact, the name manzanita in Spanish means little apple. Many California Indians learned to make a cider from these fruits.

Greenleaf manzanita is one of the most widely spread and best known of the group. Growing 3 to 8 feet tall, it bears drooping pink flowers, which are about ¼-inch long and bloom from May to June. The leathery leaves are ovate or rounded, from 1 to 2 inches long, and a bright green color, in contrast to the dull green or whitish leaves

Greenleaf Manzanita

52

of some species. Greenleaf manzanita is a typical understory shrub in open ponderosa pine woodlands.

Pinemat manzanita *(A. nevadensis)* is a spreading shrub, growing only 6 to 18 inches tall. Often it forms dense carpets on the floor of open forests, trailing over rocks and debris. The leaves, slightly over an inch in length, are elliptic in shape. The flowers, ¼-inch long, are white, sometimes with a pink tinge, and bloom in May and June in the higher elevation ponderosa pine and lodgepole pine forests.

Common manzanita *(A. manzanita)* occurs at lower elevations and grows 6 to 12 feet tall (although taller specimens have been reported). The thick, elliptic leaves are about an inch long. The drooping flower clusters are pale pink or white. It is most commonly found on the western slopes of the northern Sierra. Several other species may be found in the foothills: Mariposa manzanita *(A. mariposa)*, which grows 4 to 12 feet tall, has 1 to 2 inch long, gray, oval glandular leaves, dense clusters of pinkish flowers, and sticky fruits; white-leaf manzanita *(A. viscida)*, which grows 4 to 12 feet

tall, has whitish twigs, smooth, pale green, ovate or round leaves, pink or white flowers in open clusters, and fruits with sticky surfaces; and Indian manzanita *(A. mewukka)*, which grows 3 to 8 feet tall, has elliptical, grayish green leaves, white flowers and smooth fruits.

Range: Widespread in the mountains of the Pacific coastal states, east to Colorado, Utah, and Arizona.

SPREADING DOGBANE
Apocynum androsaemifolium
DOGBANE Family

The dogbanes, also known as Indian-hemp and Canadian hemp, constitute a small genus of plants that are rather widely distributed in the western United States. The genus is marked by the milky juice that exudes from a broken stem, by the opposite, rather thick, ovate leaves, and the small, fragrant, bell-shaped flowers.

Three species may be found in the Sierra. Spreading dogbane has very fragrant, white or pink flowers. The drooping leaves are 1 to 4 inches long and on spreading, reddish

Pinemat Manzanita   **Spreading Dogbane**

stems that are 8 to 18 inches tall. *Apocynum pumilum,* very similar in appearance, is somewhat smaller, its stems being less than 12 inches tall. There is also a slight difference in the flowers. Those of *A. androsaemifolium* have spreading tips, while those of *A. pumilum* do not. Both are found in open, dry areas, often seen along roadsides. *Apocynum cannabinum,* found in shady spots, has erect leaves and grows up to 2 feet tall.

Range: Widespread in North America.

SHOWY MILKWEED
Asclepias speciosa
MILKWEED Family

Several species of milkweed grace dry, open areas of the Sierra and are characterized by their distinctive flower arrangement and milky sap. This milkweed has rosy or purple flowers that occur in round, showy clusters. The specific name, meaning showy or spectacular, refers to this mass of flowers, which is found toward the upper end of a 1 to 4 foot tall stem. The oval or oblong, woolly leaves are 3 to 6 inches long, opposite each other on the stem, and grayish green.

Heart-leaved milkweed *(A. cordifolia)* grows up to 2 feet tall, and has broad, heart-shaped, clasping leaves that are about 6 inches long. The flowers are a dark, reddish purple. Narrow-leaf milkweed *(A. fascicularis)* has extremely narrow leaves that are often folded along the midrib. The leaves are 1 to 5 inches long and about a quarter-inch wide. They are usually in whorls of three to six and borne on a 1 to 3 foot tall stem. A particularly hairy plant, Indian milkweed *(A. eriocarpa)* is about the same size. It has creamy or purple-tinged flowers and 6-inch long, oblong leaves, that are either opposite or whorled.

These milkweeds are all found in the foothills and in lower conifer forest areas in dry, open sites, often along roadsides.

Range: California north to Washington, east to the Mississippi Valley.

Showy Milkweed

SCARLET GILIA
Ipomopsis aggregata
PHLOX Family

Also called skyrocket gilia, foxfire. This bright colored wildflower is abundant in dry openings around Lake Tahoe in early July, covering many roadside banks with brilliant scarlet. Occasionally growing among blue lupines, the bright, tubular flowers make most other wildflowers seem pale. The inch-long floral tubes have narrow lobes that spread outward from the tip of the tube and are almost flexed backward. The protruding stamens add to its attractiveness. Growing from 1 to 4 feet tall, this gilia has leaves that are divided into narrow, linear lobes. When these brilliant flowers dominate any area, their mass effect is truly spectacular. Look for scarlet gilia if you visit the upper Truckee River area in the Eldorado National Forest, Snow Creek in Yosemite National Park, or Golden Trout Creek in the Inyo National Forest.

Range: Widespread In the mountains of the western United States.

MUSTANG CLOVER
Linanthus montanus
PHLOX Family

Also called yellow-throated gilia. Most members of the *Linanthus* genus have rather small, inconspicuous flowers; mustang clover is one of the more conspicuous. It grows 4 to 24 inches tall and has leaves deeply cleft into 5 to 11 linear lobes. The flowers are in a terminal head and are tucked amid coarse, bristly bracts. The inch-long funnel-shaped floral tube is purple or lilac with a yellow throat and a dark spot on each floral lobe. It grows in open, gravelly spots and is particularly abundant in the Giant Forest of Sequoia National Park. A white-flowered form grows in foothill areas.

A somewhat smaller plant, *L. ciliatus* has short, hairy, 3 to 12 inch stems. The flowers are also in terminal heads surrounded by stiff, leaf-like bracts. The tubular flowers are about ½ inch long, with small, round, rose or purple lobes and a yellow throat. *Linanthus harknessii* has slender stems about 12 inches tall. The paired leaves are divided into three to five palmate lobes, while tiny

Mustang Clover

Scarlet Gilia

white flowers grace the top of the plant. *Iinanthus nuttallii* has numerous leafy stems, 6 to 12 inches tall. The opposite leaves, about ½ inch long, are divided to the base, making the leaves appear whorled. The one-half inch long white flowers are quite showy. They're abundant at North Lake in the Inyo National Forest.

Range: Sierra Nevada of California.

GIANT HYSSOP
Agastache urticifolia
MINT Family

The plumes of flowers adorning the giant hyssop, also known as nettleleaf horsemint, line the openings and roadways of Yosemite Valley in July. A tall fragrant plant, growing up to 5 feet tall, it occurs in a wide variety of soils and exposures—dry, gravelly, moist or sandy areas in meadows, brushlands, or open woodlands. Like other members of the mint family, the stems are square and the flowers two-lipped. The tubular flowers are white, rose or purple. Two pairs of stamens protrude from the floral tube, like spectators in a box seat. The flowers are in thimble-shaped clusters that may be 4 inches long. The flowers bloom only a few days.

Range: Southern California north to British Columbia, also in the Rocky Mountains.

MOUNTAIN PENNYROYAL
Monardella odoratissima
MINT Family

The pennyroyals are colorful and fragrant members of the Sierra wildflower community. The flowers are in bracted heads. If you take a few minutes to examine mint flowers carefully, you'll find a dainty, tubular basket with two lips, the upper erect and cleft into two lobes, the lower lip parted into three segments. Four stamens protrude from the basket. Pennyroyals can be found from lower foothill elevations up to the high windy mountain passes. Two main species occur in the Sierra.

Monardella odoratissima is widespread, with many varieties and subspecies. Found at moderate elevations, into subalpine and alpine zones, it grows 9 to 18 inches tall. Its lance-shaped leaves are about an inch long, and the flowers are a pale lavender

Giant Hyssop

Mountain Pennyroyal

or white. The leafy mountain pennyroyal grows in small clumps on dry slopes in our coniferous forests or on exposed ridges.

Western pennyroyal *(M. lanceolata)* grows at lower elevations. An erect annual, it grows 6 to 24 inches tall and has linear leaves, 1 to 2 inches long. The floral heads are an inch across and composed of reddish or purple flowers. It is quite abundant in dry areas at moderate and lower elevations.

Pennyroyal makes excellent tea and is often gathered for this purpose. The leaves can either be used fresh or dried.

Range: Sierra Nevada north into Oregon; also in the Rocky Mountains.

PURPLE NIGHTSHADE
Solanum xantii
NIGHTSHADE Family

Purple nightshade creates colorful bush-like vegetation along rocky roadsides and grassy niches, its deep green foliage contrasting with the blue flowers. These saucer-shaped flowers, a half-inch or more wide, are the texture of crinkled crepe paper. The flowers are eventually replaced by pea-shaped, green berries. The 1 to 2 inch leaves are gray and hairy, the foliage often forming compact mats. This nightshade has many subspecies, inhabiting foothills and lower elevation woodlands where it blooms in May as well as higher elevations where it blooms in late July and August.

The nightshade family includes many plants important economically, furnishing drugs, food, and decoration. Examples include the potato, tomato, tobacco, and petunia.

Range: Widespread in California.

Western Pennyroyal

Purple Nightshade

APPLEGATE PAINTBRUSH
Castilleja applegatei
FIGWORT Family

Also called painted-cup. Paintbrushes are among the most colorful and best known of our western flora. Some can be very conspicuous, especially if they cover large areas. On the eastern slopes of the Sierra, they are particularly glorious, contrasting with gray-green sagebrush. For a discussion of paintbrushes growing in wet or moist locations and the distinguishing characteristics of the *Castilleja* genus, see page 97.

C. applegatei occurs up to timberline, inhabiting a variety of plant communities, from sagebrush scrub to subalpine forests, as well as coastal mountains. It grows 8 to 20 inches tall and has hairy, glandular foliage. The inch long lanceolate leaves have crisp, wavy margins and are either entire or three-lobed. The calyx tips and bracts are scarlet (or, sometimes, orange or yellow).

A paintbrush of shorter stature, Brewer paintbrush *C. breweri* grows 4 to 10 inches tall. Its foliage is also glandular and hairy, its bracts and calyx bordered with red. It, too, occurs in dry areas, preferring stony sites or dry meadow borders near timberline.

An unusual and distinctive paintbrush, *C. nana,* is fairly inconspicuous. Only about 3 inches tall, its foliage is a grayish color. The bracts and calyxes are a dull yellow or purple, the calyx deeply cleft into linear lobes. It blooms in mid-summer in dry rocky places, between 8,000 and 12,000 feet.

Most paintbrushes are at least partially parasitic on other plants' roots. Since they have green leaves, however, they also produce their own nutrients.

Range: Mountains of California, north to Oregon and Idaho.

Applegate Paintbrush

CHINESE HOUSES
Collinsia heterophylla
FIGWORT Family

Chinese houses is well named. The pagoda-like flower clusters resemble little houses, stacked on top of each other. Blooming in the springtime at lower elevations, Chinese houses grows 8 to 20 inches tall, with opposite, lance-shaped (sometimes toothed) leaves. The flowers are nearly an inch long. The two-lipped corolla is pale lilac, pink, or purple, the upper lip being lighter than the lower. In mid-May, you'll find it blooming in the dry roadsides near El Portal in the Stanislaus National Forest. In mid-summer, another *Collinsia* may be seen in well-drained spots such as the dry meadows around Mather Ranger Station in Yosemite National Park. The flowers in this species, more often called innocence *(C. tinctoria),* are pale green or white, with purple marks in the throat. It is 8 to 24 inches tall with ovate or oblong leaves and is found up to 7,000 feet elevation.

Collinsias do not always have their flowers arranged in pagoda-like tiers or whorls. A widely distributed group known as blue-eyed Mary or blue-lips, is also encountered in the Sierra. Their two-lipped flowers have pale upper lips and deep blue lower lips. The flowers of most species are quite small, although their mass effect may be quite eye-catching. One of the larger-flowered species is *C. torreyi.* Its flowers are about ½-inch long. Found on sandy flats and banks, it grows 2 to 8 inches high and has narrow, linear leaves and erect, branching stems.

Range: Widespread in California.

Blue-eyed Mary

Chinese Houses

PRIDE OF THE MOUNTAIN
Penstemon newberryi
FIGWORT Family

No other wildflower can match the rosy red display of color put on by this penstemon, which anchors itself to crevices in rocky walls throughout the Sierra. Its most conspicuous display is probably along the granite roadcuts made by our cross-mountain highways, for here it is seen by every passing motorist. Occurring in rocky, gravelly ground from moderate elevations up to timberline, pride of the mountain has numerous stems that grow about a foot tall, making it resemble a small bush. The brightly-colored flowers bloom from June to early August.

Rivaling the scarlet gilia (see page 55) for its bright color along dry roadsides, *P. bridgesii* is abundant on the road to Onion Valley in the Inyo National Forest and to Parker Pass in the Sequoia National Forest. It grows 2 feet tall and has lanceolate leaves, 1 to 3 inches long. This narrow, inch-long, scarlet floral tube is found in the central and southern Sierra.

A white or cream-colored penstemon, *P. breviflorus* is sometimes called yawning penstemon because the upper lip is arched, the lower lip curved, giving the overall appearance of an open mouth. Its flowers have pink or purple lines and are about one-half inch long. The branching stems form loosely rounded clumps up to 6 feet tall on talus slopes below 8,000 feet elevation. Another bushy form, *P. lemmonii* has yellow flowers. The fifth stamen in this species is heavily bearded, while in yawning penstemon it is smooth.

Blue penstemon, *P. laetus,* grows 1 to 2 feet tall, and has pale blue or violet flowers an inch or more long. The foliage is a gray-green color. Blue penstemon is abundant in dry places at moderate elevations, especially where the soil has been disturbed.

Other penstemons may be noted on page 100 and 118, which also discusses the general characteristics of the group.

Range: Sierra Nevada north to Mt. Shasta.

Pride Of The Mountain

Blue Penstemon

Bridges Penstemon

60

LOUSEWORT
Pedicularis semibarbata
FIGWORT Family

This lowly plant dots the dry forest floor at middle and upper elevations. Its small yellow flowers are often hidden beneath the deeply dissected, fern-like leaves. Lousewort grows only about 4 inches tall, although its leaves may be as long as 6 inches. The yellow flowers have a hooded lip, giving it a slightly curved appearance.

Another Sierra *Pedicularis* resembles its descriptive common name. Indian warrior, *P. densiflora,* has a dense cluster of crimson-red flowers, easily portraying the brightly-colored headgear of an Indian brave. It grows 4 to 20 inches tall and is usually found on dry, sunny slopes in the foothills.

Two other species of *Pedicularis* occurring in moist areas are discussed on page 99.

Range: Mountains of southern California north through the Sierra to southern Oregon.

Lousewort

BLUE ELDERBERRY
Sambucus caerulea
HONEYSUCKLE Family

Blue elderberry graces streamsides and moist flats or slopes, its flat-topped clusters of tiny flowers blooming through most of the summer. At lower elevations in the Sierra it blooms in early June, while in more sheltered spots at higher elevations (this elderberry grows up to about 10,000 feet) it may still be flowering in late August or September. The flower clusters are 2 to 6 inches across, occasionally being even larger. These give way to blue berries, from which the specific name *caerulea*, meaning blue sky, is taken. The opposite leaves are a deep, dark green, pinnately divided into five to nine leaflets. Blue elderberry is a many-branched shrub, 6 to 12 feet tall. Sometimes it grows to the size of a small tree of 20 to 25 feet. The tart, blue berries of this elderberry can be eaten raw, although most people prefer to make them into jam, jelly, pie, or wine.

Several other species of elderberry may also be found in parts of the Sierra Nevada. In foothill areas, usually below 4,500 feet elevation, you may see *S. mexicana* blooming as early as March. Thought by some to be a variety of *S. caerulea*, its leaves have only three to five leaflets and the flower clusters are generally smaller. A red-fruited elderberry, *S microbotrys* has its flowers and fruits in pyramidal clusters. It grows in damp places at moderate and upper elevations. It is a low shrub that grows about 3 feet tall and is found in most of the Sierra Nevada, the coastal mountains, and the Rocky Mountains.

The generic name comes from the Greek *sambuke,* a musical instrument which was partly made from elderwood. The Indians often referred to this bush as "the tree of music" because of the flute-like whistle they made from the pithy stems.

Range: Widespread in the mountains of California, north to British Columbia and Alberta.

Blue Elderberry

MOUNTAIN SNOWBERRY
Symphoricarpos vaccinioides
HONEYSUCKLE Family

The hanging, bell-shaped flowers of this snowberry seem too dainty to cope with the alpine elements when this bushy shrub is found on ridgetops and mountain passes. It thrives on dry, rocky slopes, and occasionally on the forest floor at lower elevations. About 3 to 5 feet tall, this shrub has dark green, inch-long leaves. The pink or whitish flowers are tucked between the leaves at the ends of the branches. The fruits which follow are white berries, hence the common name of snowberry.

A trailing species found up to 8,000 feet elevation throughout most of the Sierra, *S. acutus,* has branches 1 to 3 feet long. It has a soft, hairy covering on the twigs and the round leaves may have irregular lobes on them. Found in shady woods and other damp places, the bell-shaped flowers are bright pink, about ¼-inch long.

Range: Sierra Nevada north to British Columbia, and east to Montana and Colorado.

PEARLY EVERLASTING
Anaphalis margaritacea
COMPOSITE Family

Pearly everlasting is a bunched or loosely tufted perennial with 1 to 2 foot tall stems and woolly white leaves. The flowers are in tight, round-topped clusters that may be up to 6 inches across. The flower-heads have yellow centers composed of tubular flowers. These heads are of two different types, female or seed-producing and male or pollen-producing. The flowers are surrounded by numerous overlapping rows of bracts which are pearly white, petal-like, and papery-textured. These last indefinitely—or are "everlasting."

The specific name means pearly and refers to the white color, which the common name also implies. When the flowers are young, the central yellow flowers are not very obvious. However, as the flower head matures, the white bracts spread, and the center flowers enlarge, becoming more conspicuous.

Pearly everlasting often grows in dense clumps on burned-over areas. The seeds are accompanied by a tuft of fine, straight

Mountain Snowberry

Pearly Everlasting

hairs, allowing them to travel great distances. Once established, the creeping rootstocks aid its rapid spread. Pearly everlasting grows mostly in open timber, rocky flats and slopes, and open meadows.

Pearly everlasting belongs to the large Composite Family. The flowers are grouped into heads, so that what appears to be a single flower is actually a "composite" of many flowers. Basically, these flowers are two shapes: flat, strap-shaped ones (for instance, those of a dandelion) and tubular ones. Some flower heads are composed entirely of strap-shaped flowers; others, like pearly everlasting, are composed of tubular flowers. Still others, such as the sunflower, have tubular flowers in the central disk area and strap-shaped flowers along the margin.

Range: Widespread in North America and Eurasia.

COMMON YARROW
Achillea lanulosa
COMPOSITE Family

Also called milfoil, wild tansy, and woolly yarrow. Common yarrow is a widely distributed plant, recognized by its fern-like leaves and white flower heads, composed of both disk and ray flowers. Growing 3 feet high, the stems are densely covered with white, woolly hairs. Flourishing in a variety of situations, yarrow is at home in brushy areas, open woodlands, dry meadows, and roadsides. It immediately invades places where the natural vegetation has been disturbed. At higher elevations, a smaller form, growing only 4 to 8 inches tall, may be found in alpine meadows and rocky fields.

The generic name *Achillea* honors the legendary Greek hero Achilles, who supposedly used yarrow to cure the wounds of his soldiers. The specific name *lanulosa* refers to the fine, woolly hairs which cover the plant and give it a grayish appearance.

Range: Widespread in North America.

Common Yarrow

Rosy Everlasting

ROSY EVERLASTING
Antennaria rosea
COMPOSITE Family

Also called catsfoot and pussytoes. A woolly perennial herb, rosy everlasting forms mats or tufts, sometimes covering several square feet. Growing at middle and upper elevations, this everlasting grows in a variety of habitats, including open, dry sites, moist meadows, alpine rock fields, and open woodlands. The small flower heads sit atop 2 to 10 inch tall stems that are covered with dense, woolly hairs, and have narrow, alternate leaves. Additional leaves are clumped at the base of the stems. This everlasting is distinguished by the rose-colored bracts at the base of each flower head.

In many everlastings the bracts are the most conspicuous part of the flower head, being white, brown, pink, or rose-colored. A species very similar to rosy everlasting, *A. corymbosa* has whitish bracts, each with a dark spot at the base. It grows in damp meadows within the subalpine forest zone to timberline through most of the Sierra Nevada. *Antennaria alpina* and *A. umbri-nella* are both smaller plants (less than 8 inches), and form mats in alpine and sub-alpine sites. The bracts of alpine everlasting have greenish-black tips, which are usually pointed. Those of *A. umbrinella* have white or pale brown tips.

Range: Widespread in western North America.

RABBITBRUSH
Chrysothamnus nauseosus
COMPOSITE Family

Also called rabbitsage or yellowbush. A late-blooming shrub, the yellow flowers of rabbitbrush produce a golden glow or halo in August and September on open dry plains and mountain slopes. A variable species with many subspecies, *C. nauseosus* is one of the most common and widespread of the genus. The cone-shaped flower heads are a bright, buttery yellow, and are located around the periphery of the shrub, which is 1 to 7 feet tall. When not in bloom, rabbitbrush is identified by its alternate, linear leaves, which are covered by fine, felt-like hairs, especially on the young

Alpine Everlasting

Rabbitbrush

outer stems. The result is an over-all white or grayish tinge. Rabbitbrush is associated with sagebrush and ponderosa and Jeffrey pine, often growing on waste areas or disturbed sites.

Range: Widespread in the drier areas of western North America.

ANDERSON THISTLE
Cirsium andersonii
COMPOSITE Family

Thistles are not usually thought of as being beautiful wildflowers. Instead, we tend to think of them as weeds which invade our pastures and meadows. Moreover, their prickly leaves are rough and sharp, further downgrading them in many person's eyes. However, most thistles are actually quite pretty. Anderson thistle is one of the most attractive to grace our mountain roadsides. Its purplish stem grows 1 to 4 feet tall and has leaves with spiny lobes and teeth. The showy blossoms appear from July to September at moderate and upper elevations in the Sierra.

Several other thistles will also be seen in the Sierra. The Sierra thistle *(C. californicum)* grows 2 to 5 feet tall and is leafy at the base. The leaves are narrow, 1 to 8 inches long, deeply cleft, and quite prickly. The disk flowers are white or cream-colored, to lavender or purple, and grouped in heads 1 or 2 inches tall. You'll find this thistle on dry slopes at moderate elevations. The bull thistle *(C. vulgare),* a weed native to Europe and quickly becoming established in waste areas in California, has purple flower heads. Its leaves grow up to 12 inches long and are armed with stout prickles. Growing up to 4 feet tall, it is common along roadsides and dry meadows at lower elevations. A peculiar thistle, found only at higher elevations in the central Sierra, *C. tioganum* has a tuft of cream-colored or yellow floral heads tucked in a rosette of basal leaves. Found in meadow borders and open forests, it occurs near timberline.

Range: Sierra Nevada north to Idaho.

Anderson Thistle

WOOLLY SUNFLOWER
Eriophyllum lanatum
COMPOSITE Family

Also called golden yarrow. This delightful little yellow-flowered composite brightens dry roadsides and rocky bluffs. A variable species, it exists in many forms. In the Sierra it is a compact, shrubby plant, usually about 5 to 11 inches tall. The leaves and stems are covered with white woolly hairs—both the genus and species names mean hairy and refer to this trait. The leaves are often so toothed or lobed that their shape would best be called irregular. Both the ray flowers and disk flowers are a vivid, golden yellow, the flower heads being about one-half inch across.

Range: Sierra Nevada north to British Columbia; also in the Rocky Mountains.

BLOOMER GOLDENBUSH
Haplopappus bloomeri
COMPOSITE Family

A compact woody shrub that blooms late in the summer, bloomer goldenbush sometimes lines Sierra passes, utilizing the water running off the highway and producing a luxurious hedge. The flower heads are clustered at the tips of the branches and have one to five ray flowers (occasionally, the flower heads have only disk flowers). The branches grow up to 2 feet tall and bear narrow, linear leaves. This rabbitbrush is found in dry, open places, from middle elevations up to timberline.

Golden aster *(H. apargioides)* is less than 10 inches tall and has toothed basal leaves 1 to 4 inches long and solitary yellow flower heads. The stems are usually decumbent, although sometimes semi-erect. Golden aster is found in dry meadows and other open areas at higher elevations and timberline. It grows from the southern central Sierra to the northern Sierra, blooming from July through September.

Whitestem goldenbush *(H. macronema)* is a low, woody shrub growing up to 18

Bloomer Goldenbush

Woolly Sunflower

Golden Aster

inches tall. The stems have numerous, inch-long linear leaves. The young stems are covered with white woolly hairs, giving rise to the common name. The yellow flower heads lack ray flowers and are composed solely of tubular flowers. Blooming from July through September, this rabbitbrush is found at timberline and above.

Range: Sierra Nevada north to central Washington.

SHAGGY HAWKWEED
Hieracium horridum
COMPOSITE Family

The shaggy-appearing leaves, densely covered with long brown or whitish hairs, are the main identifying feature of this hawkweed. Nestled in granite crevices and rocky slopes, the flowers are hardly noticed among the 3 to 4 inch long leaves. The branching stems, from 4 to 15 inches high, bear small, bright yellow flowers which bloom in July and August. A common Sierra wildflower, you'll find it on dry open rocky areas, from the montane forest to timberline.

Range: Mountains of southern California north in the Sierra Nevada to southern Oregon.

SIERRA LESSINGIA
Lessingia leptoclada
COMPOSITE Family

Creating a sea of pale purple or lavender, Sierra lessingia thrives in dry openings within the lower elevation pine forests. Look for it in the Indian Basin area of the Sequoia National Forest in early August. The lavender flower heads are composed entirely of tubular flowers. However, the outer flowers have palmate petals, giving the appearance of strap-shaped flowers. The branching stems grow up to 2 feet tall. A heavy rainstorm in mid-summer often leaves the flower heads and stems looking battered and ragged. However, they assume their perky appearance after drying in the sun.

Range: Central and southern Sierra Nevada.

Shaggy Hawkweed

Sierra Lessingia

COMMON MADIA
Madia elegans
COMPOSITE Family

A common wildflower on open, dry slopes in the foothills and at moderate elevations in the Sierra, common madia somewhat resembles a wild sunflower. The plants grow up to 30 inches tall and bear several flower heads. These showy heads are nearly 2 inches wide, both the tubular flowers of the central disk and the ray flowers being yellow. Sometimes there is a maroon or brown spot on each ray flower (as shown in the photo) making each head quite elegant. Often you will see this madia lining the roadsides in the morning. However, by noon you will be hard pressed to find the showy flower heads. This is because most of them close by mid-morning, the tips of the ray flowers curling inward. By late afternoon, they re-open.

Another common name for this group of wildflowers is tarweed, because of the sticky stems and leaves.

Range: Widespread in the mountains of California, north into Oregon.

NODDING MICROSERIS
Microseris nutans
COMPOSITE Family

A yellow-flowered plant growing about 12 inches tall, this wildflower reminds one of a slender dandelion. Like the common weed that invades many lowland gardens, the flower head is composed of yellow ray flowers and lacks disk flowers. The flower heads are nodding before they bloom, giving rise to the common name. Occurring along forest and meadow borders at moderate and upper elevations, it has linear or lance-shaped leaves on the lower part of the stem. These are 4 to 10 inches long and either entire or toothed.

Two other mountain wildflowers also resemble dandelions. The orange-flowered floral heads of *Agoseris aurantiaca* also grow on slender, leafless stems. This plant grows slightly taller, up to 20 inches, and has basal leaves 2 to 10 inches long. When fresh, the flowers are a burnt orange; however, they usually turn purple or rose with age. Growing in meadows and grassy openings, it is found at middle and upper elevations throughout the Sierra and also

Common Madia

Nodding Microseris

occurs in the Cascade and Rocky Mountains. The yellow-flowered heads of *A glauca* grow on stout stems that are 4 to 12 inches tall. It is found on dry, rocky sites, mostly on the eastern slopes of the Sierra.

Range: Sierra Nevada north to British Columbia; also in the Rocky Mountains.

CONEFLOWER
Rudbeckia californica
COMPOSITE Family

Coneflower is an appropriate name for this easily-recognized wildflower of mid-elevation openings. The flower heads are cone-shaped, usually solitary, with the brown tubular flowers elevated above the yellow ray flowers. An erect, leafy plant 2 to 4 feet tall, its leaves have a rough, hairy texture and are 2 to 4 inches long. Widely scattered throughout the Sierra, coneflower is rarely abundant in any one place. However, you might look for it at Eagle Lakes in the Tahoe National Forest and in Kings Canyon.

Closely related, the Black-eyed Susan *(R. hirta)* is found in similar places. Usually several flower heads occur near the top of the 2 to 4 foot tall stems. The ray flowers are orange or yellow, the disk flowers are a rich brown. Black-eyed Susan was originally native to the eastern states—it is the state flower of Maryland. Introduced into many areas of the western United States by early settlers, it is now common along roadsides and in dry meadows, where it blooms in July and August.

Range: Sierra Nevada north into Oregon.

Coneflower

Black-eyed Susan

CREEK GOLDENROD
Solidago canadensis
COMPOSITE Family

Also called meadow goldenrod. Growing 2 or 3 feet tall, this goldenrod occurs along streambanks and meadow borders, especially where the ground is moist. The pyramidal spray of yellow flowers appears in July or August, continuing to bloom through the fall. Many goldenrods are difficult to tell apart. However, as a group, they have many constant features. They are perennial herbs with alternate, mostly toothed leaves and erect heads of yellow flowers. Each head is surrounded by several series of overlapping bracts.

Growing above 8,000 feet, alpine goldenrod *(S. multiradiata)* rarely exceeds 12 inches in height. Common in high elevation meadows, it has lance-shaped, mostly entire leaves. It grows throughout the Sierra, Rocky and Cascade Mountains, and it is also found in Siberia and Labrador.

The yellow flowers of some species have been used to make a yellow dye, lending color to Indian crafts and clothing. The Indians also reportedly boiled the leaves to make a preparation for cuts and other wounds. In fact, the genus name is derived from the Latin meaning "to make whole."

Range: Widespread in North America.

WOOLLY MULE EARS
Wyethia mollis
COMPOSITE Family

The bright yellow flowers of mule ears, sometimes called wild sunflower, dot dry slopes and hillsides above 5,000 feet, especially on the east side of the crest. Often they mingle with sagebrush and scrub pine. The flower heads, usually solitary at the ends of the 1 to 3 foot tall stems, may be as large as 3 inches across. The oblong leaves, 7 to 19 inches long and 2 to 7 inches wide, are clumped at the base of the plant. Smaller leaves, usually less than 5 inches long, occur on the flowering stem. The leaves, especially when young, are covered with soft, white hairs, which give them a silvery appearance and inspire the common name.

Several other *Wyethia* are also found in the Sierra. Narrow-leaved mule ears *(W.*

Creek Goldenrod

Woolly Mule Ears

angustifolia) has narrower leaves (about 3 inches wide) which lack a woolly covering. This mule ears grows about 2 feet tall and is found on open slopes at lower elevations. Where both species occur, look at the flower heads. Few ray flowers adorn each woolly mule ears flower head while narrow-leaved mule ears has many (usually more than 10) ray flowers. *Wyethia elata,* a foothill species, is similar to woolly mule ears. Densely hairy and leafy-stemmed, it grows 2 to 4 feet tall. Its leaves are broad and pointed, and its flower heads have numerous ray flowers.

The genus name honors Capt. Nathaniel Wyeth, early American trapper and traveler, who crossed North America in 1834. He collected *Wyethia* and the genus was named for him.

The balsam roots are often confused with mule ears. They also have sunflower-like heads. However, in mule ears the stem leaves are quite developed; in balsam root they are reduced, or entirely absent. Two species will be considered here. A balsam root with hairy leaves and stems, *B. sagittata* has several stems up to 2 feet tall. The

woolly hairs make the younger leaves appear white. The leaves are triangular in shape. *Balsamorhiza deltoidea* lacks these soft, woolly hairs, although it may be sparsely covered with coarser hairs. The leaves, therefore, appear green, and feel rough, not smooth and soft.

Range: Sierra Nevada north into Nevada and Washington.

MARIPOSA LILY
Calochortus leichtlinii
LILY Family

Mariposa lilies are among the most attractive flowers of the lily family. The genus is best known in the western United States, where various species are also known as sego lilies, cat's ear, and star tulip. Mariposa means butterfly in Spanish and refers to the beauty of the flowers. Found in open prairies, meadows, mountain hillsides, grassy forest floors, and alpine places, they grow from a bulb and have one or two narrow leaves at the base of the stem. The flowers have three petallike sepals and three large, showy petals, each with a hairy

Balsam Root

72

gland near the base. The bulbs of most mariposa lilies are edible. Many western Indians roasted them for food.

Calochortus leichtlinii is one of the most beautiful of the mariposas. It has erect stems 8 to 16 inches tall and linear leaves. The bowl-shaped flowers are white, or, sometimes, a pale blue or pink. Each petal has a dark spot above the gland. This mariposa is found in open, stony places from middle elevations to timberline, and blooms from June to August.

One of the most common foothill mariposas, *C. venustus,* also has large, showy, bowl-shaped flowers. They are white, yellow, or purple. Each petal has a dark spot, often with a second pale spot of color above the first. It is commonly seen along the dry grassy road shoulders in the central and southern Sierra.

In dry, brushy places on the eastern slopes of the Sierra Nevada, one begins to find the sego lily, state flower of Utah, *C. nuttallii.* The flowers are white, tinted with pale purple, with a cresent-shaped purple spot above the gland.

Calochortus species with open, rather than bowl-shaped, flowers are noted on page 27.

Range: Widespread in the Sierra Nevada, east into Nevada.

SOAP PLANT
Chlorogalum pomeridianum
LILY Family

Soap plant is conspicuous wherever it grows. Its stems reach 2 to 10 feet tall and branch like a candle holder. A cluster of waxy leaves, 1 to 3 feet long and with wavy edges, is found at the base of the stems. The small white or pale purple flowers near the tip of the tall stem have green or purple veins, making them quite distinctive. The name *Chlorogalum* probably comes from the Greek *chloros,* green, and *gala,* milk or juice and refers to the sap. The specific name *pomeridianum* refers to the habit of the flowers to open in the afternoon. Soap plant grows best on dry, sunny slopes and fields below 5,000 feet, and blooms from June through August.

Soap plant has been used for glue, for soap, for poisoning fish, and for food. The

Mariposa Lily

Soap Plant

soap plant bulb contains a slippery substance. This was used by the Indians as a glue to make brushes while the fibrous material forming the outer covering of the bulb was used for the bristles. When rubbed, the inner parts of the bulb lather into a soap. The Indians also used the lather to help them catch fish. After damming a small stream and creating a lather in the water, they caught the dazed fish that came to the surface. Finally, the cooked bulb was used as food by many California Indian tribes.

Range: California north into Oregon.

WASHINGTON LILY
Lilium washingtonianum
LILY Family

Growing on the brushy hillsides of lower elevation chaparral and in mid-elevation pine forests, the Washington lily closely resembles an Easter Lily. The showy, fragrant blossoms are white, sometimes becoming pink or purple upon maturing. The spreading flowers are near the upper portion of the stem, which may be 2 to 6 feet tall. The leaves occur in several whorls along the length of the stem. At their peak in July, the flowers will still be found in some areas in early August. Watch for them along the Feather River in the Plumas National Forest in early July.

The Washington lily is a good example of the problems inherent in using common names. In northern California it is known as the Shasta lily, while in the Oregon Cascades it goes by such names as the Mt. Hood lily and the Santiam lily, depending on the local area. All of these common names are for the same plant, which has only one scientific name.

The lily family is a large group with many showy flowers (see pages 72, 106). The flower parts occur in three's or six's, making them fairly easy to recognize. The family is also rich in plants that are extremely valuable for ornamental purposes. The tulip, the mariposa, and the lily-of-the-valley are only a few examples of popular garden flowers belonging to this group.

Range: Sierra Nevada north in the Cascade Mountains to the Columbia River.

Washington Lily

74

DEATH CAMAS
Zigadenus venenosus
LILY Family

Growing from small, oblong bulbs, this plant is sometimes called white camas to distinguish it from the blue-flowered camas discussed on page 105. The 10 to 20 inch stems have plumes of white flowers near the tip and linear leaves. Usually found in grassy places that are moist at least early in the season, death camas may occur with the edible blue-flowered camas, so care should always be taken by anyone gathering camas bulbs. When not in flower, the two plants are not easy to tell apart. At certain stages of growth, the death camas can also be confused with the mariposa lily (page 72) or onion (page 107).

All parts of death camas are toxic. Poisoning of cattle or sheep usually occurs early in the summer, when the plant is still succulent. By the latter part of the summer, death camas has usually dried and so is not very palatable.

Range: Widespread in the western states.

WILD ONION
Allium campanulatum
AMARYLLIS Family

This wild onion is one of several species found in the Sierra Nevada. Growing from 2 to 12 inches tall, this species flourishes on dry road shoulders, banks, and gravelly slopes. It has two or three linear leaves, about the same length as the flowering stem. The cluster of rose-colored or pink flowers has two small leaf-like bracts beneath it. There are from 15 to 40 of these flowers, each about one-third inch long and quite delicate in appearance. A very similar species, *A. bicseptrum,* found mainly on the east slopes of the Sierra, also has rose-colored flowers. Perhaps an easy way to tell the difference is to look at the leaves. Those of *A. campanulatum* already are withering when it blooms, while the leaves of *A. bisceptrum* remain green.

A more robust wild onion, found in wet areas, is shown on page 107.

Range: California north into Oregon.

Death Camas   **Wild Onion**

BLUE DICKS
Brodiaea pulchella
AMARYLLIS Family

The *Brodiaeas* group of some 40 species reaches its greatest number and variety in California, where nearly 30 species are recorded. Some authorities list more. As a group, they have erect clusters of flowers that are tubular or funnel-shaped. Ranging in color from blue or purple to yellow and white, they are usually very colorful and attractive. Many have been cultivated. Many of the Sierra brodiaeas were prized by the Indians who dug the small bulbs (technically called corms) with sticks of mountain mahogany (page 41) and baked them in earthen ovens.

Blue dicks, also called common brodiaea, grows up to 3 feet tall and is found on dry grassy slopes and hillsides. The flowers are blue or violet, about ½-inch long, and bloom from March through May in the foothills. The grasslike leaves dry and disappear early in the summer. A more robust blue-flowering brodiaea, *B. laxa* is commonly called grass nuts or Ithuriel's spear. The last name undoubtedly calls attention to the tall, spearlike stem. The name grass nut refers to the small corm, which was prized by the Indians for its nutty flavor. Growing up to 30 inches tall, the pale purple, tubular flowers are an inch long and bloom from April through June. Common in dry places, you'll see both of these brodiaeas around the Ash Mountain area of Sequoia National Park.

Harvest brodiaea *(B. elegans)* also has blue flowers and grows in dry, grassy places. It is 4 to 16 inches tall and has narrow leaves that are about the same length. These dry by the time the flowers appear in late spring. Harvest brodiaea can easily be distinguished from grass nut, because its flowers have three functional stamens, while grass nut has six.

Brodiaeas come in colors other than blue or purple. A white-flowered species, hyacinth brodiaea *(B. hyacinthina)* is particularly conspicuous when it covers a drying meadow in mid-summer. Golden brodiaeas *(B. gracilis and B. lutea)* have yellow flowers. Each *B. lutea* flower has fine brown mid-ribs while *B. gracilis* has brown marking only on the back or undersides of the

Blue Dicks

Grass Nut

flowers. *Brodiaea gracilis* is the more dainty of the two, being 2 to 10 inches tall while *B. lutea* grows 8 to 32 inches tall. The golden brodiaeas occur on dry sandy or gravelly slopes and hillsides.

Range: Widespread in California, north to Oregon, east to New Mexico and south into Mexico.

SECTION III
WET AREAS

Golden Brodiaea

AMERICAN BISTORT
Polygonum bistortoides
BUCKWHEAT Family

Also called western bistort or mountain meadow knotweed. The flowers of this member of the buckwheat family are conspicuous components of the meadow community at Crane Flat within Yosemite National Park in early July. The white or pinkish flowers are compacted into a dense oblong cluster atop a 10 to 24 inch stalk. These stems grow from a large, fleshy rootstock that survives from year to year. Most of the long narrow leaves are found at the base of the plant, and are from 4 to 10 inches long. A few shorter leaves, however, may be found along the length of the stem. Flowering from June through August, American bistort may be found in wet meadows throughout the montane and subalpine forest.

American bistort grows in a variety of areas within western North America. In the Rocky Mountains it may be found in the alpine tundra or subalpine forests. It also grows in scattered areas along the Pacific coast. In the Sierra Nevada it characteristically grows in subalpine areas, rarely at timberline as it so often does in the Cascade Mountains. The plants found in these widespread areas differ in many subtle ways. Those in the Sierra Nevada, for instance, reproduce mainly by the spreading of underground rootstocks, while those found in the Rockies reproduce from seed.

Although the young leaves can be used as greens, the bistort root was the more important Indian food, used in soups and stews.

Range: Widespread in western North America, east across the northern continent to the Atlantic.

MONKSHOOD
Aconitum columbianum
BUTTERCUP Family

This member of the buttercup family bears little resemblance to the golden-colored flower for which the family is named. Nonetheless, monkshood is very distinctive and easy to recognize. Usually an erect plant growing 3 to 4 feet tall, it can be recognized by the tall stems, palmately lobed leaves, and peculiar flower shape. Located

American Bistort

near the tip of the stems is the showy flower of deep blue or purple (occasional white specimens have been found). There are five outer flower parts called sepals. The upper one forms a helmet. It is this hood-shaped cap that gives the flower its common name.

You will find monkshood throughout the Sierra, although it rarely occurs in great abundance in any one place. It grows in moist meadows and streamsides and is also found in damp open woods. North Lake Campground in the Inyo National Forest and the damp meadows of the Desolation Wilderness near Lake Tahoe are only a few of the places you should expect to see it.

Monkshood may be confused with the larkspur (see page 80). Both grow in similar areas and the leaves tend to resemble each other. However, the larkspur flower has one sepal forming a spur instead of a hood. Monkshood leaves may resemble those of a geranium (see page 85), making these two plants difficult to tell apart when not in bloom. However, the crushed leaves of the geranium have a very distinctive odor.

Range: British Columbia and the mountain regions of the western United States.

COLUMBINE
Aquilegia formosa
BUTTERCUP Family

One of the most common, best known, and most widely distributed of the native western columbines, *A. formosa* also is one of our more beautiful wildflowers. The showy flowers nod atop a 2 to 4 foot tall stem. Five prolonged petals are turned backward and upward, forming crimson red spurs, while the forward portions form yellow blades. This columbine may be found from sea level to timberline in the Pacific states. Associated with a wide variety of soil types, it grows particularly well along streambanks, springs, ponds, woodland openings, and moist mountain slopes. The colorful blossoms may be found from May to August, depending on elevation and latitude.

A columbine found at timberline and windy mountain passes, *A. pubescens,* has large yellow to white flowers. Forsaking the sheltered areas preferred by *A. formosa,* this columbine grows on rocky talus slopes such as those found on the flanks of Mt. Dana in Yosemite National Park and along

Columbine

Monkshood

Yellow Columbine

the trail to Piute Pass in the Inyo National Forest. Reflecting the more stringent growing conditions at these higher elevations, it is a much smaller plant.

Range: Widespread in western North America.

MARSH MARIGOLD
Caltha howellii
BUTTERCUP Family

Marsh marigolds have a world-wide reputation for their beauty and as harbingers of spring. This species is no exception. The shiny round or kidney-shaped glossy green leaves and the pure white flowers with their yellow centers create a strikingly clean appearance. The leaves may be 2 to 4 inches across while the flower itself is more than one inch in diameter. The stout, 4 to 12 inch tall stems arise from a fibrous rootstock which is invariably anchored in wet meadows, pond margins, or marshy slopes within the montane and subalpine zones of the Sierra. You can expect to see these flowers May through July, depending on elevation.

Range: Central Sierra Nevada to Oregon.

LARKSPUR
Delphinium glaucum
BUTTERCUP Family

Larkspurs are distinctive members of the buttercup family and the particular shape of their flowers make them easy to recognize. The oddly shaped flowers have five sepals that are a deep purple or blue color (occasionally, however, white flowered specimens are found). These sepals are larger and more conspicuous than the four petals. The upper sepal is spurred backward and resembles a dunce cap. Larkspurs may sometimes be confused with monkshood (see page 78), which also has a distinctive-shaped sepal.

Thirty species of larkspur are native to California. Most are extremely difficult to tell apart. They inhabit dry flats, woodlands, and ridgetops. This species, sometimes called tall mountain larkspur, is one of the few that is easily distinguished. A robust, leafy plant, growing from 3 to 6 feet tall, it is the largest of the Sierra larkspurs. Its round leaves are 3 to 5 inches wide and cleft into five to seven divisions. The flowers are clustered near the upper part of the

Marsh Marigold

tall stems. Inhabiting streambanks and wet meadows at moderate and upper elevations, it is conspicuous wherever it occurs.

Range: California north to Alaska; also in the Rocky Mountains.

PLANTAINLEAF BUTTERCUP
Ranunculus alismaefolius
BUTTERCUP Family

The buttercups are distinguished by their waxy yellow blossoms. Composed of five golden yellow petals, the glossy flowers of this species are about ½-inch across and are found along sluggish streams and in wet meadows and banks. The plant is named because of the long, tapering leaves, which resemble those of the common plantain found in most lowland lawns and fields. Most buttercups have leaves that are lobed or otherwise divided; in this species they are entire or, sometimes, shallowly toothed. These leaves are 2 to 5 inches long, the upper leaves being the shortest and narrowest. The leafy stems are erect, somewhat stout, and grow 1 or 2 feet tall. At higher elevations they may not reach a foot in height.

Several other buttercups may be encountered below timberline in the Sierra Nevada. *Ranunculus californicus,* often called common buttercup, has lower leaves that are long-petioled and divided. The lobes are coarsely toothed. Instead of consistently having five petals, however, its flowers have between 5 and 15 yellow petals. Western buttercup, *R. occidentalis,* is most often found in moist ground at lower elevations. Its flowers have five to six waxy yellow petals and are nearly an inch wide. Western buttercup grows up to 3 feet tall. A buttercup with flowers that are white with yellow centers, water buttercup *(R. aquatilis)* grows in ponds and streams at lower and moderate elevations.

An alpine buttercup is discussed on page III.

Range: Widespread in California north to British Columbia and Montana.

Larkspur

Buttercup

MEADOW RUE
Thalictrum fendleri
BUTTERCUP Family

A daintily flowered plant, meadow rue grows in moist soil alongside streams and wet seeps. The leafy stems grow 1 to 3 feet tall, with large leaves that are divided three times. You will find different types of flowers on separate plants: the male flowers, which produce the pollen, are on one plant, while the female flowers, where the seeds are produced, are on another. The male flowers are the ones that resemble hanging green tassels (pictured), while the female flowers are less spectacular.

Meadow rue grows at middle and upper elevations throughout the Sierra. Look for it along Taylor Creek when you visit the U.S. Forest Service Visitor Center at Lake Tahoe.

Range: California north to central Oregon, east to Wyoming and Texas.

SPICEBUSH
Calycanthus occidentalis
CALYCANTHUS Family

Also called sweetbush, western sweet-scented shrub. This delightful bush grows from the foothills to moderate elevations in the mountains. It is easily recognized by its glossy green leaves and the rust-red or rose-colored flowers that bloom from April to August. The common name spicebush comes mainly from the fragrant odor of the leaves, especially strong when bruised or crushed. Spicebush is usually found in fairly moist places such as canyon bottoms and stream and lake margins. One place you'll see it is along the Merced River at the Arch Rock entrance to Yosemite National Park.

Sometimes it is difficult to distinguish between a bush or shrub and a small tree. Technically a shrub is a woody plant, usually with smaller proportions than a tree, but with several branches coming from the base rather than one main trunk.

This is the only species of *Calycanthus* found in western North America; three other species of this genus are found in the south-

Spicebush

Meadow Rue

eastern United States. Indeed, the species name *occidentalis* means western, and indicates the location of this species.

Range: Coast Ranges and western Sierra Nevada of California.

WESTERN ROSEROOT
Sedum rosea
STONECROP Family

This fleshy perennial grows from a woody rootstock, from which several stems emerge. Flat, sessile, oval leaves, about a half-inch in length, are distributed along the entire length of the 2 to 6 inch tall stems, which are topped by a cluster of rose-red or purple flowers. Found from the subalpine forest zone to above timberline, this stonecrop grows in moist, rocky places. You'll find it blooming in July along cascading streams that are fed by snow melt water from higher elevations.

Other Sierra stonecrops are discussed on page 34.

Range: Sierra Nevada north to Alaska, east to Colorado.

GRASS OF PARNASSUS
Parnassia palustris
SAXIFRAGE Family

Five creamy white petals with greenish veins identify the blossoms of this showy plant. These inch-wide flowers are solitary, on the summit of 6 to 24 inch stems. The basal leaves are round or elliptic and 1 to 2 inches long. Grass of Parnassus frequents marshy spots and wet places at moderate elevations, and is found in the company of monkshood, bistort, and elephanthead. It is quite conspicuous in the damp swales around Grass Lake in the Desolation Wilderness and along Whitney Creek in Sequoia National Park.

A closely related species, *P. fimbriata* is found in boggy places in the northern Sierra. Its petals are fringed at the base, making it quite distinctive. It extends northward to Alaska.

Range: Widespread in northern and western North America.

Western Roseroot

Grass Of Parnassus

INDIAN RHUBARB
Peltiphyllum peltatum
SAXIFRAGE Family

Indian rhubarb grows 1 to 3 feet tall and has white or pink flowers, arranged loosely in a round-topped cluster. The large leaves may grow as wide as 2 feet and are usually somewhat cupped in the center. Found along fast-moving streams, Indian rhubarb grows in lower montane and subalpine forests, blooming from April to June.

The huge leaves of Indian rhubarb, which reach their greatest development after the flowers have passed, provide the basis for the plant's scientific name. Peltiphyllum (shield-leaf) refers to the leaf shape. The stem attaches to the leaf in the center, as does the handle of a shield. The name *peltatum* also refers to this shieldlike characteristic.

The common name also has significance. The young stalks can be peeled and eaten, somewhat resembling celery. The older shoots can also be eaten, after being boiled.

Range: Sierra Nevada into Oregon; also in the northern California Coast Range.

OREGON SAXIFRAGE
Saxifraga oregana
SAXIFRAGE Family

The saxifrage group is widely distributed throughout the northern temperate zone. Oregon saxifrage, one of the more common and typical forms, can be found in boggy areas, along streams, and in wet meadows at middle and upper elevations. It grows from a stout rootstock and has a basal cluster of toothed, elliptic leaves, each from 1 to 5 inches long. The glandular stems are 1 to 2 feet tall, and have a loose cluster of white flowers at the tip.

A similar plant, *S. punctata,* differs from Oregon saxifrage mainly in the outline of the leaf and smaller size. Cartwheel-shaped, the basal leaves are about as broad as they are long and evenly toothed around the edge. It can be found on moist, mossy banks and grows about 12 inches tall.

A very delicate-appearing saxifrage, *S. bryophora* is sometimes called bud saxifrage because of its budlike bulblets. These small buds resemble tiny moss plants (the name *bryophora,* meaning moss bearers, refers to these). When they fall to the ground,

Indian Rhubarb

Oregon Saxifrage

a new plant will start. Bud saxifrage grows less than 8 inches high and each stem has but a single white flower. The oblong leaves are an inch or less long. Sierra saxifrage, *S. aprica,* is found on moist stony soil from moderate elevations to subalpine and alpine areas. It has an overall purple color and is 3 to 8 inches tall. A few small oblong or spatulate leaves are at the base of the stem and the flowers are tightly clustered at the tip.

Range: Sierra Nevada north to Washington and Idaho.

RICHARDSON GERANIUM
Geranium richardsonii
GERANIUM Family

The geranium family is a large group, with about 15 different species in California alone. Some are considered weeds, while others have been widely cultivated. The name comes from the Greek word for crane (geranos) because of the imagined resemblance of the long fruit-bearing beak protruding from the center of the flower to a crane beak or bill. The geranium pistil, which has a long pointed tip, releases its seed in a very peculiar way. When the fruit is ripe, it resembles a maypole. Each section of the seedpod—the beak already referred to—separates elastically, curling from the base to the tip and releasing the seed. Geranium leaves are palmately lobed, parted like the fingers of a human hand. Early in the season the leaves may look similar to those of the larkspur or monkshood (page 80 and 78).

Richardson geranium is found in moist areas of the Sierra. Lake borders, wet meadows, or streambanks are logical spots to look for it. Growing at moderate to high elevations, it may be 1 to 3 feet tall, and has large (up to 6 inches wide) basal leaves that are parted five to seven times. The stem leaves are greatly reduced. The five-petaled flowers are white or pale pink, with purple veins, and are about an inch in diameter.

Geranium californicum grows at moderate and lower elevations in the central and southern Sierra Nevada. It is similar to Richardson geranium, but is slightly smaller (8 to 24 inches tall), with rose red

Sierra Saxifrage

Richardson Geranium

or occasionally white petals and darker veins.

Range: Southern California and northern Mexico north to British Columbia, Saskatchewan, and South Dakota.

BREWER'S CINQUEFOIL
Potentilla breweri
ROSE Family

Members of this genus are sometimes confused with buttercups, because both have yellow flowers with five petals. Close inspection, however, will show the differences. Cinquefoils have five golden yellow petals which alternate with the five green sepals located below them. Five shorter bracts alternate with the sepals. Buttercups lack these bracts between the sepals. Also see page 81.

Brewer's cinquefoil grows 12 to 20 inches tall. Its leaves have four to six pairs of leaflets crowded together and covered with soft, silky hairs. The leaflets are, in turn, divided almost to the base. This cinquefoil is found in damp meadows. *Potentilla drummondi* often grows alongside. Its leaflets are not deeply cleft, but merely toothed, and lack a hairy covering. Both are common components of moist mountain meadows and rocky basins.

Potentilla flabellifolia, commonly called fanleaf cinquefoil, is also found at higher elevations, growing up to 12 inches tall. The leaves of this species remind one of the strawberry—three wedge-shaped leaflets comprise a leaf.

Another cinquefoil, *P. fruiticosa,* is common in some alpine areas and lodgepole pine forests. Called bush cinquefoil, it is a woody shrub, 1 to 4 feet tall, with leaves composed of three to seven narrow leaflets. Since it is the only woody cinquefoil known to occur in the Sierra, it is easily identified and is especially conspicuous when the bright yellow flowers are blooming.

Range: Sierra Nevada north into southern Oregon.

Brewer's Cinquefoil

Bush Cinquefoil

CINQUEFOIL
Potentilla gracilis
ROSE Family

Also called five-finger. More than 25 species of *Potentilla* occur in California; several are found in the Sierra. This variety is one of the more common and widespread, also being found in the Cascade Mountains. The cinquefoil is sometimes confused with the buttercup (see page 86 for a description of the differences). The name cinquefoil is probably derived from the French word *cinque,* five, and a medieval English word *foil,* leaf. This refers to the five fingerlike leaflets characteristic of many cinquefoils.

About one-half inch across, the flowers of this species are extremely attractive. The five, bright yellow floral petals are somewhat heart-shaped, a small notch being in the outer edge. The leaves are mostly basal and are composed of five to seven leaflets. These leaves are palmately divided, meaning each of the leaflets originates from a common point, like the fingers of a hand. This cinquefoil is extremely variable, growing 15 to 30 inches tall, from lowland areas to timberline. Generally, it will be found in moist places such as streambanks and wet meadows.

Potentilla glandulosa has pinnately compound leaves, meaning that the leaflets are arranged on both sides of the petiole or leaf stalk. Growing up to 30 inches tall, this cinquefoil occurs in dry or moist openings. The flowers are pale yellow rather than the bright golden yellow of *P. gracilis.* Although usually found at moderate and lower elevations, it is known to occur up to 12,000 feet.

Range: California north to Alaska, east to Colorado and the Dakotas.

THIMBLEBERRY
Rubus parviflorus
ROSE Family

Thimbleberry is one of the most widespread members of this genus, which includes the wild and cultivated blackberries and raspberries. First collected and named by the botanist Nuttall (see page 17 for more about Nuttall) on the shores of Lake Huron, it occurs west of the Great Lakes and in all the states of the far West, from Alaska south to Chihuahua, Mexico.

Thimbleberry

Cinquefoil

Thimbleberry has showy, white flowers with five petals, which are thin and crinkled like crepe paper. The leaves are alternate on the stem, 3 to 12 inches wide, and have three to five pointed lobes. Thimbleberry grows on moist, shaded sites, along streams and cool draws, and on wooded hillsides, under open clumps of ponderosa and lodgepole pine. Sometimes forming dense, almost solid stands, it is a conspicuous plant when blooming in June and July. The name thimbleberry is derived from the shape of the berry. The juicy, reddish fruit, resembling the cultivated raspberry, is rather bland. Nonetheless, it provides a refreshing snack for hikers passing along the way.

Range: Widespread in western North America.

WOOD ROSE
Rosa woodsii
ROSE Family

The rose is an erect, trailing, or climbing shrub, often with prickly stems. The alternate leaves are usually compound, and the leaflets have toothed edges. The five-floral petals (rarely four, six, seven, or eight) are red, pink, or sometimes, yellow. The fleshy, round fruit, known as a hip, is red. This hip, rich in vitamin C, can be made into a tasty jelly. Also, chopped and steeped in hot water, it makes a good tea.

Wood rose is a stout, erect shrub, 3 to 9 feet tall. Its leaflets are scarcely an inch across and very pleasantly scented, as are the 1 to 2 inch wide flowers. It grows in damp coniferous forests, particularly in the eastern Sierra.

Range: Widespread in the western United States; the form found in the Sierra Nevada is usually considered to be *R. woodsii* var *ultramontana*.

Wood Rose

BROAD-LEAF LUPINE
Lupinus latifolius
PEA Family

Lupines comprise a well-known and widespread group of western plants, being variously known as blue pea, quakerbonnets, and bluebonnet (the state flower of Texas). Probably the most commonly used name, however, is lupine. Lupines are characteristic of a wide range of sites or habitats, extending from the plains to mountain foothills and meadows, from open slopes to wet streambanks. Most conspicuous when in full bloom, large masses often cover an entire area with vivid color. A general listing of lupine characteristics and the species found in drier habitats are noted on page 46.

This species is a robust, bushy plant, growing up to 4 feet tall, although usually shorter. The lavender or blue flowers are one-half inch long. The 4 to 8 inch long leaves have five to twelve leaflets that are oblong to lanceolate in shape. It thrives in moist soil, along a spring or seep area, and may be seen along roadsides where it utilizes the extra moisture that runs from the hard pavement.

Range: California north through the mountains of Oregon and Washington to British Columbia and Alaska.

OREGON SIDALCEA
Sidalcea oregana
MALLOW Family

The mallows are some of the prettier components of wet meadows, especially since they bloom into August, when other meadow flowers have begun to fade. The flowers of this mallow are often closely clumped together at the tip of the stems, which are from 1 to 5 feet tall. The round leaves are 1 to 4 inches wide, the basal ones with five to seven shallow lobes and the upper stem leaves deeply divided into about seven narrow lobes. The subspecies shown below, *S. oregana* ssp. *spicata,* is common throughout the Sierra and can be seen in early August at Round Meadow in Sequoia National Park or in early July at Hope Valley in the Toiyabe National Forest.

Mallows found in dry areas are discussed on page 47.

Range: Sierra Nevada north into Oregon and Washington.

Broad-leaf Lupine

Oregon Sidalcea

ST. JOHN'S WORT
Hypericum formosum
ST. JOHN'S WORT Family

Common in meadows and along streamsides, this yellow-flowered plant belongs to a family widely distributed in tropical and temperate regions. Only a few species, however, occur in the western United States. One of these, Klamath weed *(H. perforatum),* originated in Europe and has become an aggressive weed species in many of our western rangelands.

This species is known for its five-petaled, yellow flowers, accentuated by slender, erect stamens, and oblong, inch-long leaves, which are dotted with black spots along the margins. The flowers are about a half-inch wide and are loosely clustered at the upper ends of the stem, which grows 10 to 20 inches tall. The flowers bloom from June to August and are found mainly in the damp openings of mid-elevation coniferous forests.

Another member of this genus found in similar locations is tinkers penny, *H. anagalloides.* It is a trailing plant from 2 to 7 inches long and forms small mats in wet areas from California to Montana and British Columbia.

Range: Southern California north to Montana and British Columbia.

EVENING PRIMROSE
Oenothera hookeri
EVENING PRIMROSE Family

The flowers of the evening primrose open in the evening and close the next morning when hit by warm sunlight. Nonetheless, in the early hours of the day, before the flowers wither, they are quite conspicuous. They are large and showy, being 2 or 3 inches wide. When first open, they are pale yellow; however, they become an orange or reddish color as they wilt. The flowers are at the top of a stout, reddish stem, 3 to 6 feet tall, although most higher elevation plants are only 3 or 4 feet tall.

Evening primrose is a biennial. This means that the primrose seed produces a rosette of basal leaves the first growing season. Only during the second year does the flowering stalk grow and produce the cluster of large yellow flowers familiar to so

St. John's Wort

Evening Primrose

many mountain visitors. The plant is often branched and produces flowers throughout the entire summer. It is found in moist areas at moderate elevations.

Range: Widespread in California, north into Oregon and east to Colorado.

Mountaineers and Indians used this dogwood as a tobacco substitute, using the green inner bark as the smoking substance.

Range: Sierra Nevada north to Alaska and east across northern North America to the Atlantic; also found in the Rocky Mountains.

CREEK DOGWOOD
Cornus stolonifera
DOGWOOD Family

Creek dogwood hardly looks like its large relative, the flowering dogwood (see page 17). Instead of growing to tree-size, it remains a shrub, rarely larger than 10 feet tall. Rather than large showy bracts surrounding the flower cluster, this dogwood has small white flowers, borne in a round-topped cluster that is 1 or 2 inches across. Forsaking the shade of forest edges, it abides by streams, sometimes forming a dense thicket. One of this dogwood's real beauty features is most obvious in the winter, when it and other streamside plants have lost their foliage. The winter stems are a deep red color, adding a splash of brightness to any winter setting.

Creek Dogwood

COW PARSNIP
Heracleum lanatum
PARSLEY Family

One of the most conspicuous of the parsleys, cow parsnip derives its scientific name very logically. The species name, *lanatum,* refers to the hairy covering found on most of the stem. The name *Heracleum,* derived from Hercules, refers to its mighty size. The stout stems grow 8 or 9 feet tall, although 4 or 5 feet is more common. Everything about the cow parsnip is rather large. The flowers are clustered in flat-topped heads 5 to 12 inches across. The leaves, which are divided into three deeply toothed leaflets, are also of large proportions. They are 5 to 20 inches across and their general form reminds one of rhubarb. Found in moist openings and along streambanks at middle elevations, cow parsnip blooms from May to August.

The tender leaves and flowering stalks, being sweet and aromatic, were collected by Indians and used for food. This was usually done in the spring and early summer before the flower clusters opened. Cattle are also very fond of it because the foliage is green and palatable all summer long. In some places where it is extensively grazed, it has become difficult to find.

Range: Widespread in North America; also found in the Kurile Islands and Siberia.

RANGERS BUTTONS
Sphenosciadium capitellatum
PARSLEY Family

Rangers buttons, also called button parsley, swamp white heads, and button parsnip, belong to a distinctive and wide-ranging family. Members of the parsley (or carrot) family have compound leaves, stems which are usually hollow, and flowers borne in clusters called umbels. An umbel resembles an inside-out umbrella, with all the erect ribs (the flower stems) originating from a common point. Depending on the length of these "ribs" the flower cluster may be rounded or flat on top. Many commercially important plants belong to this group. Caraway, dill, parsnip, celery, and carrot are only a few. Other members of this family are noted on page 50 and 51.

Found along streams and in other moist

Cow Parsnip

Rangers Buttons

places, rangers buttons resembles cow parsnip (page 92). However, its flowers are not clustered in large flat-topped umbels. Instead the tiny white flowers are in dense fuzzy balls about ½-inch in diameter. The entire umbel is about 4 inches across. Flowering from July to August, rangers buttons grows 2 to 5 feet tall at moderate and upper elevations.

Range: Southern California north to northeast Oregon and Idaho.

ALPINE LAUREL
Kalmia polifolia
HEATH Family

The kalmias are a rather small group of plants, with only about a half dozen species in North America. While alpine laurel is generally small and of low stature, one eastern species is a small tree, sometimes 20 feet high. Alpine laurel, also called alpine kalmia or dwarf laurel, is a low, evergreen shrub, usually only 4 to 12 inches high. Fairly common in moist, boggy sites at high elevations, it usually grows in full sunlight, its pink saucer-shaped flowers dancing in

the seemingly ever-present breeze. The slender branched stems have sessile inch-long leaves which have their edges rolled under, making them seem quite narrow.

The Sierra plant is usually assigned the varietal name of *microphylla* because of the small size of its leaves.

Range: Widespread in the higher mountains of western North America.

LABRADOR TEA
Ledum glandulosum
HEATH Family

Nestled along rocky streambanks, usually in the partial shade of lodgepole pine, Labrador tea is found throughout the Sierra. If you hike along the Tuolumne River near Glen Aulin in Yosemite National Park in early July, you'll find many of these shrubs in bloom. Labrador tea grows 2 to 5 feet tall, and has round-topped clusters of white flowers at the ends of the branches. The leathery, evergreen leaves are oval or oblong, about 2 inches long, and occur alternately on the stem. The leaves have smooth edges and their undersides are dotted with

Alpine Laurel

Labrador Tea

tiny glands, hence the species name *gland-ulosum.* Often the leaves have a fragrant odor of their own, especially when crushed.

Range: Widespread in western North America.

SHOOTING STAR
Dodecatheon jeffreyi
PRIMROSE Family

Also called bird-bill. Shooting stars are recognized by their four or five purple petals, united at the base but divided into linear segments which are curved back over the rest of the flower, exposing the erect stamens. Three species are commonly found in the Sierra.

Jeffrey shooting star *(D. jeffreyi)* grows 1 to 2 feet tall in wet mountain meadows and has a basal cluster of leaves, each from 2 to 15 inches long. Five to 15 nodding flowers grace the top of each stem. At higher elevations in the central Sierra a distinctly smaller plant may be found, *D. jeffreyi* var. *pygmaeum.* Usually only 4 to 8 inches tall, it has thick, short basal leaves that are 1 to 2 inches long.

The pygmy form may be confused with alpine shooting star *(D. alpinum),* which grows about a foot tall and has strap-shaped leaves, 1 to 5 inches long. Despite the name, it grows in moist meadows throughout the subalpine Sierra forest, not just at upper elevations. The two species can be distinguished by close examination of the individual flower stem: Jeffrey shooting star has small glands or hairs, while alpine shooting star does not.

At higher elevations in the southern Sierra, *D. redolens* is encountered. It is quite glandular and grows 10 to 24 inches tall. Its flowers have five stamens; the other shooting stars discussed here usually have four stamens.

Range: Sierra Nevada north to Montana and Alaska.

EXPLORER'S GENTIAN
Gentiana calycosa
GENTIAN Family

Gentians are commonly associated with mountain meadows, each lending itself to the beauty of the setting. This genus has

Shooting Star

Explorer's Gentian

erect herbs with showy flowers, the floral petals joined to make a somewhat funnel-shaped blossom. The four or five-lobed flowers are blue, violet, green, or white.

Explorer's gentian, *G. calycosa,* found from the Sierra Nevada to Montana and British Columbia, has simple, leafy stems with rounded inch-long leaves. Growing 5 to 15 inches tall, explorer's gentian has deep blue, funnel-shaped flowers, each about an inch long. The five floral lobes are connected by a bluish membrane with several teeth. The flower may be green dotted, adding to its beauty and charm.

Sierra gentian, *G. holopetala,* is one of the most common, being found in damp meadows within the montane, subalpine, and alpine zones. The four-lobed flowers are dark blue, 1 to 2 inches long. Each flower is on a single stem, although several stems may make up a single plant. The lobes of the green calyx are usually dark ribbed. A very similar gentian, one-flowered or hiker's gentian *(G. simplex)* has but a single stem and the calyx lobes lack the dark rib. Both bloom from July through September.

A gentian found from Alaska to Lower California, *G. amarella,* grows 2 to 20 inches tall. An erect, leafy plant, it has several half-inch long, blue flowers, each with five oblong lobes.

Alpine gentian *(G. newberryi)* is one of the more elusive Sierra wildflowers. Growing 1 to 3 inches tall, it has several stems that are prostrate or decumbent at the base. The inch long floral tube is pale blue or white, and dotted with green. Because of its small stature, you must look carefully for this gentian. It is often hidden among the sedges and grasses of the meadows where it grows.

Range: Sierra Nevada north in the mountains to British Columbia and Montana.

DEERS-TONGUE
Frasera speciosa
GENTIAN Family

Also called green gentian. Most of our mountain gentians are rather small plants with tubular blue or white flowers. This gentian has flat, star-shaped greenish-white flowers, each 1 to 2 inches wide, that are found in the axils of the leaves. A robust plant, it stands 3 to 6 feet high, and has

Hiker's Gentian

Deers Tongue

leaves that are 4 to 10 inches long. These are opposite each other or grouped in whorls. Deers-tongue can be found in grassy spots and meadows within lodgepole pine or red fir forests, nearly up to timberline.

Range: Sierra Nevada north to Washington; also in the Rocky Mountains.

MOUNTAIN LUNGWORT
Mertensia ciliata
BORAGE Family

Lungworts are also called languid ladies (because of their drooping leaves and flower clusters) or bluebells (a name which is more properly reserved for members of the genus *Campanula.*) Lungworts as a group have smooth, alternate leaves which are sometimes covered with fine hairs that cause them to have a bluish cast. The nodding, tubular blue flowers are quite showy. Blooming from June to August, lungwort grows up to five feet tall. The half-inch flowers are a pale pink in bud, turning blue as they mature, and fading pink again. Mountain lungwort grows in clumps in wet

or moist areas, usually associated with willow, butterweed, and monkeyflowers.

Range: Sierra Nevada into southern Oregon and east to Nevada.

WHITE HEDGENETTLE
Stachys albens
MINT Family

White hedgenettle is well named, for it is covered with soft, woolly white hairs. As the plant matures, these often become matted and cob-webby. Most hedgenettles are rather rank, coarse plants, falling into disfavor for their resemblance to stinging nettles, which are actually in another family. White hedgenettle has white or pinkish tubular flowers that are two-lipped, the upper lip erect and the lower lip spreading. Although the individual flowers are rather small, they are actually quite pretty and ornate. White hedgenettle grows 1 to 4 feet tall in moist woodlands and meadows below 8,000 feet throughout the Sierra. One spot to look for it is at Raven Meadow in the Sequoia National Forest.

Similar in over-all appearance, rigid hed-

Mountain Lungwort

White Hedgenettle

genettle *(S. rigida)* has stiff hairs and rose or purple colored flowers, instead of soft hairs and white flowers. A taller plant, it grows 2 to 5 feet high and is also found in moist spots.

Range: Mountains of northern California to the southern Sierra; also the White Mountains.

INDIAN PAINTBRUSH
Castilleja miniata
FIGWORT Family

Also called painted-cup. The paintbrushes are among the most colorful components or our mountain flora. Most occur in varying shades of red, pink, or, sometimes, yellow. There are some 200 species of paintbrush, with over 30 of these occurring in California. Although the paintbrush group is easy to recognize, individual species are often difficult to identify. This is because the most showy and conspicuous part of a paintbrush is not the floral petals, but the ragged-edged bracts found below each flower and the floral sepals. These bracts are reminiscent of a paintbrush, recently dipped in a paint bucket. The tubular corolla (united petals) is often small and fairly inconspicuous, and is tucked down between the brightly colored bracts.

In this paintbrush, which is one of the commonest and most widely distributed of Sierra *Castillejas,* the leaves are smooth and mostly entire, lanceolate in shape, and from 1 to 2 inches long. The stems are erect, 2 to 3 feet tall, and support large red spikes. This paintbrush is found in moist areas from lower elevations up to timberline.

Meadow paintbrush *(C. lemmonii)* has several simple stems, 4 to 8 inches tall, and is noted for its purple flowers and bracts. Its narrow leaves are 1 to 2 inches long, the upper ones usually divided. Found in moist meadows in the subalpine forest zone, it occurs from the central Sierra northward to the southern Cascades. *Castilleja culbertsonii* is very similar. However, it has fewer stems. Like meadow paintbrush, it grows in wet, high mountain meadows. However, it is not so widespread, being found in alpine areas from Tulare and Inyo counties to Mono and Madera counties.

Range: Widespread in western North America.

Indian Paintbrush

Meadow Paintbrush

LEWIS MONKEYFLOWER
Mimulus lewisii
FIGWORT Family

These pink blossoms, which resemble the cultivated snapdragon, grow along moist seeps and streams. The showy flowers, usually in pairs, are 1 to 2 inches long and bloom from mid-June to early September. The tubular flower is two-lipped, with five spreading lobes, two turning up and three turning down. Since this species is so widespread, a great deal of variability occurs in both its foliage and in its flowers. For instance, even though the flowers are pale pink in the Sierra Nevada, they are deep rose-colored in the Cascades. Both the common name and the specific name are references to the well-known explorer, Captain Meriwether Lewis.

Crimson or scarlet monkeyflower *(M. cardinalis)* is closely related. It has large, velvety, 2-inch long flowers, which are quite showy and were introduced into Europe by the explorer-botanist, David Douglas, for garden cultivation. Found along streams and springs from California and New Mexico to Alaska, it grows 2 to 4 feet tall and has sticky, hairy leaves.

There are many other species of *Mimulus* in the Sierra. Some are of small stature; others are quite large and showy. All have tubular, two-lipped flowers. Although the Lewis and crimson monkeyflower have rose or red flowers, many others have yellow flowers.

Common monkeyflower *(M. guttatus)* has inch-long, bright yellow flowers with a red or brown-dotted throat. Found in wet places, it grows 1 to 3 feet tall and has toothed leaves that are about an inch long. A widespread and variable species, it is often quite a bit smaller at high elevations. Growing up to timberline, it occurs from Mexico to Alaska and is also found in the Rocky Mountains.

Mimulus tilingii is quite similar, also having yellow flowers. However, while common monkeyflower may have many blossoms on each plant, *M. tilingii* usually has only one to three. Growing in wet places from 6,000 to 11,000 feet, its leaves are often cool and slimy to touch.

Growing close to the ground in wet areas, *M. moschatus* has yellow flowers that are

Crimson Monkeyflower

Lewis Monkeyflower

Common Monkeyflower

about 1 inch long. Its leaves are covered with dense, white hairs.

The dainty primrose monkeyflower *(M. primuloides)* has a single, yellow flower atop its slender 1 to 6 inch tall stem. All the leaves, which are wedge-shaped, elliptic, or ovate, are basal. Sometimes the leaves have long, upright hairs, which glisten like exquisite jewels when covered with dew.

Range: Widespread in the western United States.

ELEPHANTHEAD
Pedicularis groenlandica
FIGWORT Family

Also called elephantflower, fernleaf, elephanttrunk, and lousewort. The common name elephanthead is a direct reference to the oddly-shaped reddish or purple flower. The floral petals are united to form a two-lipped affair. The upper lip is strongly bent and extended, forming the elephant trunk. The lower lip is three-lobed, the two outer lobes bent back to form the elephant's flapping ears. Upon close inspection it takes little imagination to see the flower stalk as a mass of elephantheads, swaying in the mountain breeze. The showy spike of flowers, on a 6 to 24 inch stem, is most often found in moist, open meadows, from mid-elevations to timberline. The leaves, mostly basal and up to 5 inches long, are lance-shaped, but deeply dissected so that they resemble a dainty fernleaf. This distinctive plant usually blooms in July and August.

A miniature elephanthead, *P. attolens,* is found in drier sites. The flower spikes in this species are covered with white hairs and the plant itself is smaller, growing between 6 and 16 inches tall. It, too, is found from mid-elevations to alpine areas, blooming from May through September.

Range: Widespread over much of northern and western North America.

Primrose Monkeyflower

Elephanthead

MEADOW PENSTEMON
Penstemon rydbergii
FIGWORT Family

Also called whorled penstemon. This penstemon dots moist or drying meadows in the montane and subalpine forest zones, its deep purple flowers arranged in whorls around the upper portion of the stem. The tubular flowers are about ½-inch long and bloom from May through August, depending on the elevation. Meadow penstemon grows 8 to 24 inches tall.

A very similar-appearing species, Sierra penstemon *(P. heterodoxus)* is found in dry subalpine meadows and slopes and at timberline. Blooming in July and August, its deep purple flowers also occur in whorls, but often there is only a single whorl atop each stem. Its flower clusters are glandular, while those of meadow penstemon are smooth. It is also shorter, growing only about 8 inches tall.

Where both species are found in a single meadow, for instance in Tuolumne Meadows, meadow penstemon grows in the lower, moist areas, while Sierra penstemon inhabits the drier meadow margins.

Range: Sierra Nevada north to Washington and Idaho.

BEARBERRY HONEYSUCKLE
Lonicera involucrata
HONEYSUCKLE Family

Also called bearberry, inkberry, twinberry, and skunkberry. A freely branching shrub, bearberry honeysuckle adorns shady streamsides and moist glens, its paired yellow flowers supported on their own stems. The flowers are cradled by broad, hairy bracts, which enlarge, turn red, and become more conspicuous as the inkblack berries form. The twigs and branches of this honeysuckle are also paired and carry 2 to 6 inch long oval leaves. Bearberry honeysuckle is one of the best known and more common honeysuckles to be found in the western United States. It grows 2 to 5 feet tall, although occasional bushes 10 feet or more tall are encountered.

In contrast, *L. conjugialis* grows 2 or 3 feet tall and is often called dwarf honeysuckle. It has thin, oval leaves 1 to 3 inches long and small (about a quarter inch), dark

Bearberry Honeysuckle

Meadow Penstemon

purple flowers with protruding stamens. It grows on moist banks and meadows.

Range: Coastal areas and mountains, from Alaska to Mexico.

ALPINE ASTER
Aster alpigenus
COMPOSITE Family

Also called dwarf purple aster. Common in high mountain meadows and alpine boulder fields, this little aster dots moist openings. The structure of its leaves and stems give it an identifying characteristic. Its narrow, often grasslike, deep green leaves are mostly basal, from 2 to 6 inches long, and tapered toward the base. The 2 to 16 inch tall stem, however, is horizontal before becoming erect, appearing to arise from the side of the basal cluster of leaves. The floral heads have yellow centers and pink or pale purple ray flowers. Often this aster grows in small colonies, thus covering an extensive area. It is also found in the Cascade Mountains, the form found in the Sierra generally being called *Aster alpigenus* ssp *andersonii*.

Aster peirsonii is found in subalpine and alpine meadows and moist rocky sites. It is a dwarf plant, with basal rosettes of leaves and stems that are less than 3 inches tall. The violet or purple flowers bloom from late July to September near timberline and above in the southern Sierra Nevada.

Asters are named for the resemblance of the rayed floral heads to stars. A large genus, over 20 species of aster occur in California.

Range: Northern North America, south into the Sierra Nevada, Cascade and Rocky Mountains.

Alpine Aster

WESTERN MOUNTAIN ASTER
Aster occidentalis
COMPOSITE Family

Western aster adorns the borders of drying meadows and ponds or shaded forest edges, blooming in August and into September when other wildflowers have faded and the grasses and sedges have dried and turned brown. The stems are 8 to 20 inches tall and have oblanceolate leaves along their entire length. The flower heads contain violet or lavender ray flowers and yellow disk flowers. These showy heads are 1 to 2 inches wide and may be found at moderate elevations throughout the Sierra Nevada.

Long-leaved aster, *A. adscendens,* is most commonly found east of the Sierra crest. A good place to look for it is on the trail to Glen Alpine in the Desolation Wilderness. Its slender stems usually grow from 8 to 30 inches tall and have linear leaves in the middle and oblanceolate leaves at the base. It, too, has violet ray flowers and yellow or gold disk flowers.

Asters are sometimes confused with the fleabanes, also members of the Composite Family. Generally speaking, fleabanes bloom early in the summer while asters bloom later in the summer and fall. However, this is not a good criterion to use because mountain summers are usually very short, and summer merges into fall rather quickly, especially at higher elevations. The ray flowers of fleabanes are usually more numerous and narrower than those of asters. Once you recognize several individuals, this characteristic should help you distinguish the two groups. The distinguishing characteristics of the Composite Family are noted on page 64.

Range: Sierra Nevada north to Alaska; also in the Rocky Mountains.

Western Mountain Aster

ASTER FLEABANE
Erigeron peregrinus
COMPOSITE Family

Also called wandering daisy, daisy fleabane. This fleabane is commonly found at moderate and upper elevations, where it grows in moist meadows and alongside meandering streams. You'll find it blooming along the headwaters of the Tuolumne River, in the meadows adjacent to the Tioga Pass Road in Yosemite National Park in July and August. It is felt by many to be the most showy and common fleabane of the higher mountains. It has stems up to 30 inches tall, although most are from 12 to 24 inches tall. The lower portion of the stem is quite leafy, with clumps of oblong leaves 3 to 8 inches long. The flower heads are an inch or more across and have violet or purple ray flowers and yellow disk flowers. This fleabane is widely distributed in the western parts of North America. The form found in the Sierra is generally referred to as *E. peregrinus* ssp. *callianthemus.*

Several other showy fleabanes are found at moderate and lower elevations. *E. strigosus,* also called daisy fleabane or branching daisy, has smaller flower heads, less than an inch wide. The numerous ray flowers are white or pale purple. The stems, which are 10 to 30 inches tall, branch at the top and have 2 to 4 inch long bristly leaves. This fleabane is not native to California, but was introduced from the eastern U.S. It is found in moist meadows at moderate and lower elevations and blooms from June to early August. Brewer daisy *(E. breweri)* and leafy daisy *(E. foliosus)* are both found in drier places. They have blue or purple ray flowers and yellow disk flowers. Brewer daisy has erect or trailing stems 4 to 12 inches long. The leaves are oblong or rounded, about an inch long, and have stiff hairs. It grows in rocky areas between 5,000 and 10,500 feet elevation. Leafy daisy grows on grassy hillsides or dry slopes, usually below 6,000 feet elevation. Its stems grow 1 to 2 feet tall and have narrow, linear leaves that are 1 to 2 inches long. The flower heads are about an inch in diameter.

Range: Widespread in the mountains of western North America.

Aster Fleabane

BIGELOW SNEEZEWEED
Helenium bigelovii
COMPOSITE Family

This sneezeweed is an attractive and common component of mid-elevation Sierra meadows. A place to look for it is Quaking Aspen Meadow in the Sequoia National Forest. Standing 2 to 3 feet tall, its dome-shaped flower heads are easy to recognize. The golden-brown disk flowers are surrounded by yellow or bronze rays which droop downward. Lance-shaped leaves, 4 to 10 inches long and about an inch wide, adorn the stem.

Near timberline, one is likely to encounter *Helenium hoopesii,* orange sneezeweed. It is a leafy stemmed plant with oblong leaves. Both the ray and disk flowers are burnt orange or yellow, the floral head being 2 or 3 inches across. Orange sneezeweed begins blooming in early July, at the edge of melting snowbanks. In August, it is still blooming, often in the same area but in places where the snow lingered longer.

Range: Sierra Nevada and Coast Ranges of California, north into Oregon.

ARROWLEAF BUTTERWEED
Senecio triangularis
COMPOSITE Family

Patches of arrowleaf butterweed, also called groundsel, lend vivid color to a landscape—and are indicative of a moist slope or seep. The leafy stems of this robust plant may grow as tall as 6 feet, although 3-foot plants are more common. Both the specific name and part of the common name allude to the arrowlike shape of the leaves. The name butterweed refers to the yellow flower heads. Although occurring from moderate elevations to timberline, butterweed grows best in the cool, higher elevations, where it often forms extensive patches. There it flowers from mid-July through August.

Another *Senecio* found in moist sites is Clark groundsel *(S. clarkianus).* Found in mid-elevation meadows in the central and southern Sierra, it grows 2 to 4 feet tall and has oblong or lance-shaped, not triangular, leaves. These are 2 to 8 inches long and have deeply cut leaf margins. *S. pauciflorus,* blooms in July and August in damp meadows. It has orange flower heads which usually lack ray flowers.

Bigelow Sneezeweed

Orange Sneezeweed

The general characteristics of the *Senecio* group are discussed on page 26.

Range: Widespread in the mountains of the western United States, north into Alaska.

LEICHTLIN'S CAMAS
Camassia leichtlinii
LILY Family

This camas has deep blue flowers composed of three sepals and three petals that look so alike the average observer assumes that the flower has six petals. These are arranged symmetrically. This distinguishes Leichtlin's camas from common camas *(C. quamash)* which is also found in the Sierra. In the common camas five of the floral parts are erect or horizontal while the sixth turns downward.

Found in subalpine meadows, camas was one of the most important of all native plants for the Indians. Camas fields were cherished and held by various Indian families, who guarded the coveted bulbs from their rivals. After the seeds were ripe, the bulbs were dug and baked or roasted for at least 24 hours. Many settlers also learned to use the camas bulbs, and even made pies from them. Care was always taken when digging camas, however, because the bulbs look like those of the white-flowered death camas (see page 75). Even Indians were known to have been poisoned from mistaking the death camas for the edible camas.

Range: Coast Ranges and Sierra Nevada, north to British Columbia.

Arrowleaf Butterweed

Leichtlin's Camas

SIERRA LILY
Lilium kelleyanum
LILY Family

Its delicate orange flowers bobbing in the faintest breeze, the Sierra lily adorns streambanks and moist places. Looking very much like many of the cultivated lilies of our lowland gardens, Sierra lily is one of the larger wildflowers of our mountains and is usually found in the graceful company of elephanthead and bog orchid. Growing 2 to 6 feet tall and having oblong leaves that are in whorls near the upper portion of the stem, Sierra lily has nodding orange flowers, distinguished by their recurved petals.

Alpine lily, also called small leopard or tiger lily *(L. parvum),* is recognized by bell-shaped flowers that are erect or horizontal, not drooping or nodding. The flowers are rose-colored, orange, or yellow, and have maroon spots. Found in moist areas, it is especially common in partially shaded glens near the roadsides around Lake Tahoe. Leopard lily *(L. pardalinum)* grows 3 to 8 feet tall and forms large groups along streambanks and wet areas at lower elevations. The nodding flowers are yellow or dark red and have petals 2 or 3 inches long. Like those of the Sierra lily, the flower petals are recurved backward. However, Sierra lily flowers are much smaller, usually being less than 2 inches long.

A showy lily that grows in open, dry places, is discussed on page 74.

Range: Sierra Nevada to northern California.

CORN LILY
Veratrum californicum
LILY Family

Also called false hellebore. This tall, coarse-leaved plant is plentiful in marshy spots, along streambanks, and in wet meadows. The stout stem grows from 3 to 6 feet tall and has large, parallel-ribbed leaves. However, it is the plume of white flowers that is most conspicuous. The drooping blossoms appear in July and August throughout the Sierra. Corn lily usually grows in small clumps, a trait making it even more notable. The common name refers to the general resemblance of the plant to cultivated corn. Another name often used

Sierra Lily

Alpine Lily

is skunk cabbage; however, that name is more properly given to a yellow-flowered plant growing at lower elevations along the coast.

Corn lily has been reported as poisonous, the roots and young shoots being considered the most toxic. As the plant grows and matures, however, it becomes less toxic and is usually considered harmless after a frost. Hellebore roots have been used as an insecticide. Dried and made into powder, they were sprinkled on garden plants to rid them of insect pests. The alkaloids found in this genus have been used medicinally to slow the heartbeat and lower the blood pressure.

Range: Widespread in the western United States.

SWAMP ONION
Allium validum
AMARYLLIS Family

This common and conspicuous onion grows in wet places throughout the Sierra. It lines shaded streams or grows in open marshes. Its prevalence is attested to by place names such as Onion Valley in the Inyo National Forest. A robust plant, it grows tall enough to let its cluster of rose-red flowers stand above the surrounding rushes and reeds. The flattened flowering stems grow 1 to 3 feet tall and have grasslike leaves up to 2 feet long. These leaves emit an unquestionable onion odor (the specific name means strong). Take a small nip of a leaf and you will taste the strong flavor. These leaves (and the bulb) were used as seasoning in stews, soups, and other pioneer dishes. You'll find plenty of wild onion not only at Onion Valley, but also at such places as Mineral King in the Sequoia National Forest and along Sagehen Creek in the Tahoe National Forest.

There are many species of wild onion in the Sierra. Page 75 describes two species common in drier places.

Range: Sierra Nevada north to Idaho and British Columbia.

Corn Lily

Swamp Onion

WESTERN BLUE FLAG
Iris missouriensis
IRIS Family

A patch of this pale blue iris adds beauty to any mountain meadow. Growing in small clumps, it is quite abundant in moist areas up to timberline throughout the Sierra. You'll find a lush display of it around North Lake in the Inyo National Forest. The large, showy blue flowers are 2 or 3 inches across and appear on stems 8 to 30 inches tall. The broad, flat leaves grow about the same height. This flower blooms from May through August, depending on elevation, and its leaves stay green until after the bloom. Then, if the meadow has begun to dry out, the plant also dries, leaving the three-parted seed pod in place of the flower.

A smaller, less robust iris occurs in dry pine forests at lower elevations on the western slopes of the Sierra. *Iris hartwegii* rarely exceeds 12 inches in height, and has narrow, linear leaves. Its flowers range in color from lavender to pale yellow or cream to a rich golden yellow. The golden yellow form is especially conspicuous around Pinecrest Lake in the Stanislaus National Forest.

Range: Widespread in western North America.

BLUE-EYED GRASS
Sisyrinchium bellum
IRIS Family

This small wildflower of lush openings is indeed well-named. The narrow grasslike leaves are barely different from those of the surrounding grasses and sedges. The purple flowers appear as tiny eyes peering upward. Growing 6 to 24 inches tall from a cluster of fibrous roots, blue-eyed grass blooms throughout the summer. The stalked flowers protrude from a pair of sheathing bracts and are yellow at the base. A wide-ranging plant, blue-eyed grass is extremely variable and is often divided into several subspecies.

Sisyrinchium elmeri is a yellow-flowered species found in the San Bernardino, the Sierra Nevada, and the Trinity Mountains. It occurs in marshy places.

Range: Widespread in the Pacific States.

Western Blue Flag

Blue-Eyed Grass

SIERRA REIN ORCHID
Habenaria dilatata
ORCHID Family

A dense spike of white flowers with long spurs identifies this orchid, which is found in boggy places through most of the Sierra. Often it is found along wet roadsides and lake margins, where it mingles with camas and shooting stars. The linear leaves resemble those of the surrounding grasses and sedges. The thick, leafy stems grow 1 to 3 feet tall and bear half-inch long white flowers near the tip. The upper petals of the flowers are arched while the spurred lip is flat and reinlike. The name *Habenaria* comes from the Latin, *habena* meaning rein, because the lip looks like the rein used with horses.

A green-flowered bog orchid, *H. sparsiflora*, is somewhat similar, but has fewer flowers spread along the upper portion of its 1 to 2 foot tall stalk.

Range: Widespread across northern North America and in the western United States. The form found in the Sierra Nevada is generally assigned to the variety *leucostachys*, meaning white-spiked.

SECTION IV

ALPINE AREAS

Sierra Rein Orchid

109

MOUNTAIN SORREL
Oxyria digyna
BUCKWHEAT Family

This delicate, alpine perennial is recognized by the round or kidney-shaped basal leaves that emerge from a woody base. The green or reddish flowers are only a quarter-inch long and hang from the tip of the upright, 2 to 10 inch tall stems. The thin, flat fruits are also conspicuous, being a deep rose color.

A plant that is widely distributed in the mountains of the western United States, mountain sorrel is well known to most hikers and campers who venture above timberline. Found nestled on rocky slopes between 8,000 and 13,000 feet in elevation, it is confined to moist crevices where it is protected from drying, gusty winds. We often think of the wind-swept alpine zone as being rather desertlike and dry. However, slow-melting snowbanks provide a constant supply of moisture, and irregular topography creates shelter for a variety of plants. You might look for alpine sorrel when you're hiking along the rocky alpine expanses around Piute Pass and Tioga Pass in late July and August.

The generic name *Oxyria* is derived from a Greek word meaning sour, and refers to the acid juice of the leaves. Hikers find mountain sorrel leaves a refreshing snack.

Range: Alaska east to Greenland; southward on the higher mountains of North America. This is a circumpolar species, also being found in the mountains of Europe and Asia.

DWARF LEWISIA
Lewisia pygmaea
PURSLANE Family

Found only in the higher elevation basins and slopes, this little wildflower is often overlooked by hikers who explore the Sierra high country in June and early July. A low growing plant, it usually hugs the ground, the linear basal leaves sprouting from a thick, fleshy root (characteristic of many lewisia) and extending beyond the flowering stems. The pink or white flower, consisting of six to eight petals, is about one-half inch in diameter. This lewisia usually

Mountain Sorrel

Dwarf Lewisia

110

grows in soil kept moist by nearby melting snow and may conspicuously dot an area one week, only to disappear by the following week.

Very similar, Nevada lewisia *(L. nevadensis)* is also found in moist soil. However, it may grow at lower elevations too, being found in ponderosa pine forests in the springtime. Where the two occur together, you can distinguish them by carefully looking at the two sepals, located beneath the floral petals. The sepals of dwarf lewisia are toothed and have purple glands, almost appearing purple-fringed. Those of Nevada lewisia are not fringed or glandular.

Several other species of lewisia are discussed on page 31.

Range: Sierra Nevada north to Idaho.

ALPINE BUTTERCUP
Ranunculus eschscholtzii
BUTTERCUP Family

Alpine buttercup basks in the sunshine at timberline and above, usually in the melt water of a retreating snow bank. Growing up to 6 inches tall, its glossy petals are a bright golden yellow. The rounded leaves are deeply three-lobed, with the middle lobe sometimes being further divided. It is the flower, however, that attracts attention. When in bloom, it covers the leaves and is quite conspicuous, the individual flowers being 1 to 2 inches across. Look for this little buttercup in rocky meadows and alpine fell-fields. It can be found blooming in places such as Emerald Lake in the John Muir Wilderness by early July; other areas, where the winter lingers and the snow remains longer, this buttercup saves its spurt of growth and flowering until mid-August.

The buttercups are a large group of wildflowers that are usually found in wet or boggy areas. The flowers are most easily recognized by the shining yellow petals, which usually number five and have a waxy coating which gives them a glossy sheen.

Lower elevation buttercups can be found on page 81.

Range: Sierra Nevada, north to Alaska; also in the Rocky Mountains.

Alpine Buttercup

DRABA
Draba lemmonii
MUSTARD Family

A compact crown of bright yellow flowers identifies this typical member of the alpine flora. It may be found in many of the high elevation passes and basins—look for it among the rocky crevices in Humphreys Basin or on the rocky slopes of Mt. Dana. The dense cluster of stems rise only a few inches from the ground. The leaves, less than one-half inch wide and oblong with a narrow base, produce a dense cushion of foliage. The golden flowers are in a tight cluster and appear in July and August. A short, twisted pod bearing the seeds follows the fading of the flowers.

Many explorers and botanists collected plant specimens in the mountains of California during the late 1800's. John G. Lemmon visited Yosemite in 1878, having come to California several years earlier after being released from a Confederate prison when the Civil War ended. He became an avid plant collector, discovering this one on Mount Lyell. Other plants named for Lemmon include *Castilleja lemmonii* (page 97) and *Penstemon lemmonii* (page 60).

Range: Sierra Nevada of California; also the Wallowa Mountains of northeastern Oregon.

ALPINE PRICKLY CURRANT
Ribes montigenum
SAXIFRAGE Family

This small shrub grows in the partial shade of lodgepole and whitebark pine near timberline. A densely branched, scraggly shrub, it grows 1 or 2 feet tall and has alternate leaves with five deeply cut lobes. The small reddish brown or rust colored flowers (about an eighth inch long) are clustered beneath the leaves along the spiny stems and are thus not very conspicuous. The red berries which follow are covered with soft, edible bristles.

Range: Sierra Nevada north to British Columbia; also in the Rocky Mountains.

Draba

Alpine Prickly Currant

ALUMROOT
Heuchera rubescens
SAXIFRAGE Family

This dainty little plant frequents rocky cliffs and crevices in the upper portions of the subalpine zone. The clusters of hairy-stemmed, rounded, inch-long basal leaves nestle against a rocky shelf, while the slender flowering stems grow up to 12 inches above the leaves. The tiny, cup-shaped flowers are white or pale pink, and appear to be dancing in the continuous alpine breeze.

Most authorities consider the Sierra plants to be *H. rubescens* var. *alpicola*. A much more robust-appearing plant, *H. micrantha* grows in sheltered rocky areas at lower elevations. Its flowering stems grow 12 to 24 inches tall.

Most alumroots have stout, woody bases or underground rootstocks, many of which have an alumlike taste, resulting in the common name.

Range: Mountains of California and Nevada.

ROCK FRINGE
Epilobium obcordatum
EVENING PRIMROSE Family

Nestled amid the crevices of dry slopes and ridges, rock fringe grows near timberline. About 6 inches tall, it has bright red or rose flowers that are about an inch in diameter and have four notched, heart-shaped petals. Small, ovate leaves, opposite each other, are crowded onto the short stem. When in bloom, the brightly-colored flowers appear to peek out from between rocks and boulders. You might look for it when hiking in the vicinity of Sonora Pass in the Eldorado National Forest, Mt. Whitney in the Inyo National Forest, and Castle Pass in the Tahoe National Forest.

Range: Sierra Nevada north to Idaho.

Alumroot

Rock Fringe

RED HEATHER
Phyllodoce breweri
HEATH Family

This flower is one of the most delightful alpine flowers to be found in the Sierra. Not elusive or rare, it is easily found near timberline and on open rocky surfaces.

You'll find red heather, affectionately called bryanthus by John Muir, in the acid soil around high elevation lakes and marshy spots or clinging to moist rocky surfaces. Most hikers in July and August will encounter this mat-forming plant in subalpine and timberline areas. However, it also occurs as a ground cover in shady hemlock and fir forests. The pink, bell-shaped flowers, about one-half inch long, appear soon after the snow melts. A woody plant, red heather never grows very tall. Its thin stems are 6 to 12 inches high and covered with short, narrow, evergreen leaves, which circle the stems. The protruding stamens make the flowers even more dainty.

Range: High mountains of California north to Mt. Shasta.

WHITE HEATHER
Cassiope mertensiana
HEATH Family

Found in rocky banks and crevices near timberline, the white heather, also called cassiope greets those who sojourn in the high country. Its flowers are white (sometimes pale pink) and the leaves are pressed flat against the stems, in tiers, to form overlapping scales. Like the red heather and many other alpine plants, white heather is a plant of low stature, the stems being only 4 to 12 inches tall. Instead of being erect, the white flowers nod from the tips of the creeping stems. John Muir referred frequently to cassiope, leading many to believe it was his favorite alpine flower. He carefully described cassiope as bringing life to otherwise desolate looking rocky mountain slopes, saying that its presence alone made the mountains sing.

Range: Sierra Nevada north to Alaska and Montana.

White Heather

Red Heather

SIERRA BILBERRY
Vaccinium nivictum
HEATH Family

Finding ripe huckleberries while hiking in the mountains is one of the rare rewards of visiting the Sierra. Bilberries are fairly common in the high country and the fruits are both sweet and tasty. However, because of their small size and the eager appetites of most small rodents, ripe bilberries are hard to find.

The Sierra bilberry, also called dwarf blueberry, is a tufted, sprawling shrub. It grows only a few inches tall and is found in high elevation meadows above 7,000 feet, usually near a retreating snowbank. The small oval leaves, barely an inch long, may cover rocky areas with a green carpet. The little pink flowers hide among the leaves, as do the berries, which ripen in August or September. Actually, it is in the late summer and early fall that these dainty plants are most conspicuous. It is then that the leaves turn a brilliant scarlet, painting the otherwise drab rocky slopes with color.

The western blueberry *(V. occidentale)* is a low growing shrub, usually found in moist meadows or along stream banks in subalpine areas. The white or pink urn-shaped flowers bloom in June or July. The blue-black fruits ripen in late August or September. They are about one-quarter inch in diameter, and have a white bloom on their surface. This blueberry is found in the Sierra Nevada and Cascade Ranges of the Pacific states and also in the Rocky Mountains.

Range: Sierra Nevada north to Mt. Shasta.

SIERRA PRIMROSE
Primula suffrutescens
PRIMROSE Family

Seeing a patch of these rose or purple-colored flowers is, indeed, breath-taking. Composed of a floral tube with a yellow throat and five widely-spreading, deeply notched lobes, Sierra primrose waves in the mountain breeze, usually not far from a retreating snowbank. Sierra primrose might even be considered "snowbank dependent." It is most often seen in a north-facing, protected ravine or hollow, where it can

Sierra Bilberry

Sierra Primrose

depend on the slowly melting snow for constant moisture.

The flowers are on a leafless stalk, 1 to 4 inches high, while the evergreen leaves are clustered at the base. Wedge-shaped, they are toothed at the tip and about an inch long.

Sierra primrose is an erratically distributed plant. More common in the southern Sierra, it is usually found in isolated colonies, although each may be quite extensive and contain hundreds of plants. As one goes north, the primrose is encountered less frequently; nonetheless, it grows in isolated places such as Basin Peak near Donner Pass and Round Lake in the Plumas National Forest.

Range: Sierra Nevada and the mountains of northern California.

SPREADING PHLOX
Phlox diffusa
PHLOX Family

Spread over open rocky and sandy spots from moderate elevations to timberline, this phlox can carpet large areas with its pink, white, or lilac blossoms. The half-inch wide flowers occur at the tips of short, branching stems that are densely covered with short, pointed leaves. Sometimes the flowers are so dense they completely cover the leaves beneath them. The woody, prostrate stems grow 4 to 12 inches long, forming thick mats. Depending on elevation, phlox blooms from June to August. A plant that closely resembles the spreading phlox, granite gilia *(Leptodactylon pungens)* is also found on rocky slopes throughout the Sierra. It, too, is a compact, leafy plant. In phlox, however, the leaves are opposite each other on the stem and entire (without notches or lobes); *Leptodactylon* leaves are arranged alternately on the stems and are cleft into lobes. The flower is also different. Granite gilia has a funnel-shaped flower and is a creamy white, yellow, or pink color; phlox flower lobes spread abruptly, at right angles to the flower tube.

Range: Sierra Nevada north into the high mountains of the Northwest.

Spreading Phlox

SKY PILOT
Polemonium eximium
PHLOX Family

Thought by many to be the finest and most beautiful Sierra wildflower, sky pilot is strictly a plant of alpine high country and is rarely found below 10,000 feet. Its crown of brightly-colored, fragrant blue flowers draws attention in its otherwise stark surroundings. One must wonder, upon finding an extensive colony growing amid the rocks of an alpine slope how the plants survive or anchor themselves in the seemingly nonexistent soil.

Sky pilot can be mistaken for no other wildflower—and rarely has any competition for its chosen habitat. Its deep blue flowers have rounded lobes and are clustered in a circular ball. The leaves, 1 to 4 inches long, consist of numerous leaflets, all crowded on the elongate leaf so that it resembles a slender, fuzzy caterpillar. These leaves are sticky and have a musky odor. The stems from the previous year's leaves are usually found near the base of the green growth.

Range: Central and southern Sierra Nevada.

TIMBERLINE PHACELIA
Phacelia frigida
WATERLEAF Family

Tucked amid rocky crevices and slopes, timberline phacelia rarely grows more than 10 inches tall. Its foliage appears gray, being covered with stiff hairs. The lance-shaped leaves are entire, not lobed or separated as those of the phacelias discussed on page 24 and found at lower elevations. The pale lavender or almost white flowers are tightly coiled in spikes reminiscent of a violin fiddlehead. These bloom from July through September. The coiled flower cluster is typical of phacelias. Timberline phacelia grows above 7,000 feet elevation and can be found on most high Sierra passes and plateau areas above timberline.

Range: Sierra Nevada north into southern Oregon.

Sky Pilot

Timberline Phacelia

DAVIDSON'S PENSTEMON
Penstemon davidsonii
FIGWORT Family

Also called creeping penstemon, beard-tongue. Growing on rocky, open slopes at timberline and above, this penstemon produces an exquisite display of tubular, purple flowers that are so large they often cover and obscure the leaves. You'll find large mats of this penstemon in such places as the rocky slopes of Kearsarge Pass. A rock-hugging plant, its ovate evergreen leaves may only be a quarter-inch long while the flowers are over an inch long. It grows 4 to 6 inches tall and, despite this small size, is sometimes considered a shrub because the stems grow from a woody base.

There are many penstemons in the Sierra, and, although they are hard to tell apart (also see pages 60, 100), the group itself is easy to recognize. The flowers are a double-lipped basket, the upper lip consisting of two lobes, the lower lip of three. The word penstemon comes from the Greek *pente,* five, and *stemon,* stamen. The stamens are inside the double-lipped basket. Only four of the stamens bear pollen, while the fifth is sterile. This penstemon was named for Professor George Davidson, who collected specimens of the plant on Mt. Conness north of Tioga Pass in 1890.

Davidson's penstemon exhibits many of the qualities required to survive at timberline. The plant is short, which helps it avoid the brunt of the wind and fully utilize windbreaks such as rocks, hollows or boulders; it has evergreen leaves, allowing it to begin growth and photosynthesis as soon as the snow melts; its stems are closely grouped, allowing them to act as wind breaks and shelter for each other; and its flowers are a rich, dark color, aiding its absorption (rather than reflection) of warmth-giving sunshine.

Range: Sierra Nevada north in the mountains to British Columbia.

Davidson's Penstemon

CUT-LEAVED DAISY
Erigeron compositus
COMPOSITE Family

This compact little fleabane, known by its leaves which are divided or cut along their tips, is found only by those who are willing to hike into high alpine areas. The leaves, crowded onto short, thick stalks that are only a few inches tall, and flowers are tucked into the safety of rocky crevices at timberline. The nearly inch-wide flower heads cover the leafy mat, the ray flowers being pale purple or nearly white, the disk flowers being yellow. Several other alpine fleabanes may be encountered in the high country. Also found in rocky areas, *E. vagus* has similar appearing flowers. The leaves, however, are mostly three-lobed. Dwarf daisy *(E. pygmaeus)* and Sierra daisy *(E. petiolaris)* are also found in rocky places near timberline. However, their leaves are entire, instead of being cut or divided. Their flower heads have blue or purple ray flowers. Dwarf daisy is a compact plant with mostly basal leaves, and barely grows 2 inches tall. It occurs in the central Sierra and adjacent Nevada. Sierra daisy grows 2 to 10 inches tall. Although most of the egg-shaped leaves are clustered at the base, a few narrow leaves may also be found on the flowering stems. This dainty fleabane is found in alpine areas from Mt. Whitney to Lake Tahoe.

Most Sierra fleabanes have flower heads with both ray and disk flowers (see page 64 for a discussion of Composite Family characteristics). The tubular center (disk) flowers are usually yellow; the numerous petal-like ray flowers are pink, purple, or white. Rarely are they yellow or orange.

Range: Sierra Nevada north to Alaska and east to Greenland; also in the Rocky Mountains. The plant found in the Sierra is generally considered to be *Erigeron compositus* var. *glabratus*.

Cut-leaved Daisy

119

ALPINE GOLD
Hulsea algida
COMPOSITE Family

Also called alpine sunflower, this is truly a plant of high windy places. Rarely found below 10,000 feet elevation alpine gold is at home on open, exposed ridges and rocky swales. Growing 4 to 16 inches tall, alpine gold has golden colored flower heads that are 1 to 2 inches wide and bloom from July through August. The basal leaves are oblong and irregularly toothed. More noticeable, however, is their soft, sticky feel and strong odor. Although not abundant, alpine gold is locally common in many alpine places. Often the upright posture and golden color, so characteristic and vivid when the flower first blooms, becomes battered by mid-summer storms, resulting in the tattered appearance shown in the photo below.

Another Sierra hulsea, *H. vestita,* is also found in open, dry places. However, it also grows at lower elevations. Occurring in the southern Sierra, it stands 12 inches tall and has woolly-white leaves clustered at the base. Each stem bears a single yellow flower head, which may be tinged with purple. A dwarf form barely reaching 2 inches in height occurs above timberline.

Range: Mt. Whitney, north in the Sierra Nevada and into Montana.

SILVER RAILLARDELLA
Raillardella argentea
COMPOSITE Family

Growing on open slopes of granite and pumice ridges, silver raillardella is a small plant, growing less than 4 inches tall. A single flower head of orange disk flowers sits atop the short, leafless stem—the leaves are basal and are covered with soft, silvery hairs. Silver raillardella is often found in colonies so that a large area may be covered with these soft, silvery leaves, which identify the plant even when it is not in bloom. The flowers appear in July and August, depending on elevation and exposure, and are fairly common in scattered areas above timberline. You might look for them while hiking in the vicinity of the Hall Natural Area in the Inyo National Forest or Castle Pass in the Tahoe National Forest.

Alpine Gold

Silver Raillardella

Often growing nearby, *R. scaposa,* is quite similar. However, it lacks silvery hairs. Its green leaves are mostly basal and the leafless stems are between 2 and 16 inches tall. Although the flower head usually consists entirely of disk flowers, occasionally ray flowers are also present. This raillardella grows in dry, rocky or gravelly areas and along dry meadow borders from moderate elevations to timberline.

Range: Sierra Nevada north into the Cascade Range of Oregon.

GLOSSARY

Green-leaved Raillardella

SOME TERMS YOU MAY WANT TO KNOW —AN ILLUSTRATED GLOSSARY

Botanical terminology has been minimized in this book. Plant descriptions are in terms familiar to most readers. However, sometimes, for the sake of accuracy, exact terms have been used. When you encounter such a term in the text, refer back to these pages for a definition and/or illustration.

The root. The root is the underground or downward portion of the plant. Roots are of two main types: they may be *fibrous,* with slender, threadlike branches; or they may be *taproots,* consisting of a single, stout root and few branches. *Rootstocks* are underground stems that are rootlike and often produce additional stems at their joints.

The stem. The stem grows upward from the root and has leaves, flowers, and fruits. Leaves are usually arranged in one of several ways along the length of the stem:

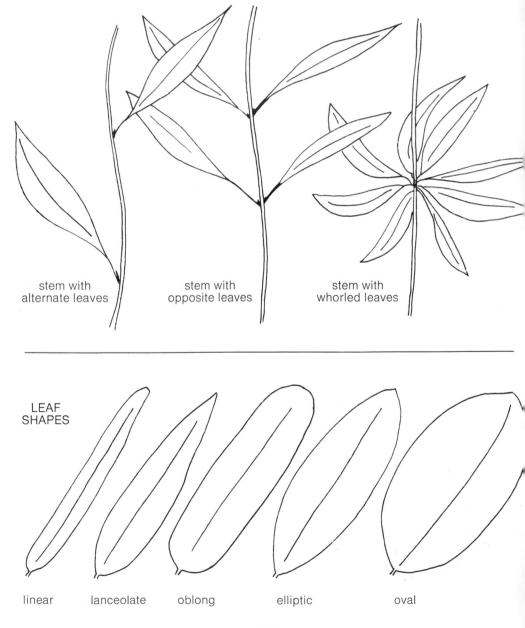

stem with
alternate leaves

stem with
opposite leaves

stem with
whorled leaves

LEAF
SHAPES

linear lanceolate oblong elliptic oval

LEAF TYPES—Leaves may be simple or compound, and come in a variety of shapes.

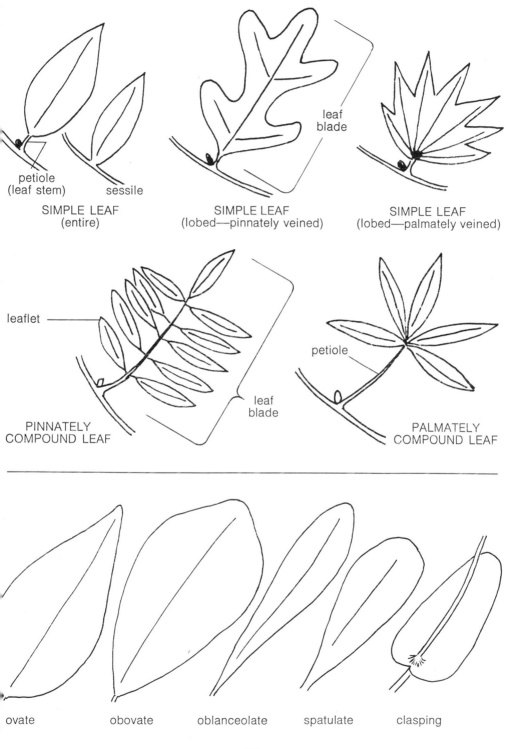

petiole
(leaf stem)   sessile

leaf
blade

SIMPLE LEAF
(entire)

SIMPLE LEAF
(lobed—pinnately veined)

SIMPLE LEAF
(lobed—palmately veined)

leaflet

petiole

leaf
blade

PINNATELY
COMPOUND LEAF

PALMATELY
COMPOUND LEAF

ovate   obovate   oblanceolate   spatulate   clasping

The flower. The flower is the part of the plant involved with reproduction. Flowers may be of several types, some containing only the female or seed-producing organs, some containing only the male or pollen-producing organs, others containing both. Some flowers lack the showy petals many associate with flowers. A typical flower is shown in the diagram below.

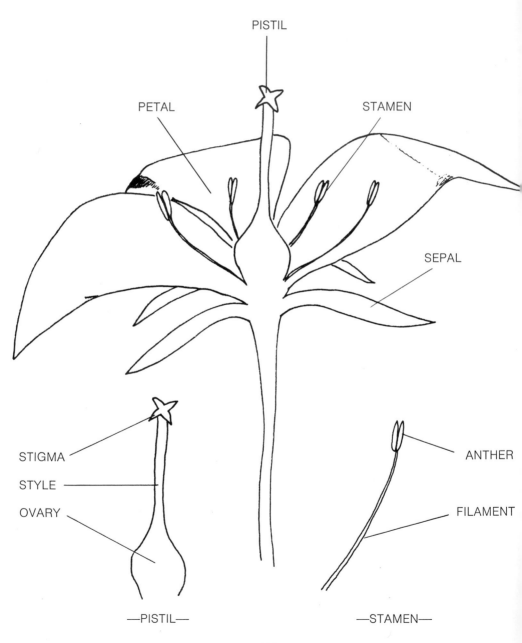

PISTIL

PETAL

STAMEN

SEPAL

STIGMA

STYLE

OVARY

ANTHER

FILAMENT

—PISTIL—

—STAMEN—

GLOSSARY

Alternate—occurring singly, not opposite.

Annual—lasting only one year.

Basal—at the base, e.g. leaves at the base of a plant.

Bract—a small, modified leaf, usually at the base of a flower or cluster of flowers.

Calyx—the outer circle of flower parts (sepals).

Ciliate—hairy along the margin.

Corolla—the inner circle of flower parts (petals).

Decumbent—lying down or growing along the ground.

Desiccate—to dry up.

Disk flower—the central, tubular flowers of a composite, e.g. the yellow flowers in the center of a daisy.

Elliptic—oblong, with rounded ends.

Habitat—the place where a plant grows.

Head—a very close, compact cluster of flowers.

Lanceolate—lance-shaped, much longer than broad, but broader at the base and tapered at the tip.

Leaflet—one of the parts of a compound leaf.

Linear—long, narrow and with parallel sides.

Oblanceolate—lance-shaped, but broad at the tip and tapered at the base.

Obovate—shaped like an egg but with the broadest part at the tip.

Opposite—occuring directly across from each other.

Ovate—shaped like an egg, with the broadest part at the base.

Parasite—obtaining its nutrition by living in or on another organism.

Pedicel—the stalk or stem of a single flower.

Pendant—hanging.

Perennial—lasting from one year to the next.

Petal—one of the floral parts, usually colored.

Petiole—the leaf stalk.

Pistil—the central seed-bearing organ of a flower.

Prostrate—growing flat on the ground.

Ray flower—the flat, elongate flowers of a composite, e.g. the white marginal flowers of a daisy or the yellow flowers of a dandelion.

Rootstock—an underground rootlike stem.

Rosette—a collection of leaves arranged circularly around the base of a plant.

Saprophyte—a plant growing on dead organic matter.

Sepal—parts of a flower below the petals, usually green.

Sessile—stemless.

Simple—one piece, as opposed to compound (in leaves).

Spatulate—narrow at the base and wide at the tip.

Spur—saclike or tubular projection from a sepal or petal.

Stamen—the floral organ bearing the pollen.

Subspecies—geographically or physiologically isolated population of a larger-ranging species.

Taproot—a stout, vertical root.

Whorled—three or more similar organs radiating from the same spot, e.g. whorled leaves.

SELECTED REFERENCES:

Abrams, Leroy, *Illustrated Flora of the Pacific States,* Stanford U., California Stanford University Press, 1940, 1950, 1951, 1960. 4 Vols.

Ball, Edward K., *Early Uses of California Plants,* Berkeley, U. of California Press. 1972.

Hall, Harvey M. and Carlotta C., *A Yosemite Flora,* San Francisco, Paul Elder and Co., 1912.

Hood, Bill and Mary, *Yosemite Wildflowers and their Stories,* Yosemite, California Flying Spur Press, 1969.

Forest Service, U.S.D.A., *Range Plant Handbook,* Washington, D.C. U.S. Government Printing Office, 1937.

Munz, Philip A. and David D. Keck, *A California Flora and Supplement,* Berkeley, University of California Press, 1973.

Pool, Raymond J., *Flowers and Flowering Plants,* New York, McGraw-Hill Book Co., Inc., 1941.

Smiley, Frank J., *A Report upon the Boreal Flora of the Sierra Nevada of California,* Berkeley, California, University of California Press, 1921.

Thompson, Steven and Mary, *Wild Food Plants of the Sierra,* Berkeley, Dragtooth Press, 1972.

126

Editor:
Thomas K. Worcester

Design:
Dean McMullen